BREATHE BETTER, SLEEP BETTER

How to use the breath to get a great night's sleep

Anandi, The Sleep Guru

BALBOA.
PRESS
A DIVISION OF HAY HOUSE

Balboa Press books may be ordered through booksellers or by contacting:

Balboa Press
A Division of Hay House
1663 Liberty Drive
Bloomington, IN 47403
www.balboapress.com
1 (877) 407-4847

Because of the dynamic nature of the Internet, any web addresses or links contained in this book may have changed since publication and may no longer be valid. The views expressed in this work are solely those of the author and do not necessarily reflect the views of the publisher, and the publisher hereby disclaims any responsibility for them.

The author of this book does not dispense medical advice or prescribe the use of any technique as a form of treatment for physical, emotional, or medical problems without the advice of a physician, either directly or indirectly. The intent of the author is only to offer information of a general nature to help you in your quest for emotional and spiritual well-being. In the event you use any of the information in this book for yourself, which is your constitutional right, the author and the publisher assume no responsibility for your actions.

Any people depicted in stock imagery provided by Thinkstock are models, and such images are being used for illustrative purposes only.
Certain stock imagery © Thinkstock.

Print information available on the last page.

ISBN: 978-1-5043-6775-2 (sc)
ISBN: 978-1-5043-6776-9 (e)

Balboa Press rev. date: 11/21/2016

This book is dedicated to my life teachers, Yogi Vishvketu, who helped me find the light, and Georg Feuerstein, who inspired me to write this book.

With gratitude from the depth of my heart

Disclaimer

Any information found in this book is for general educational and informational purposes only. It is not intended nor otherwise implied to be medical advice. You should always consult your doctor or other health-care professional to determine the appropriateness of this information for your own situation or should you have any questions regarding a medical condition or treatment plan.

Contents

Testimonials

"Anandi is a dedicated student and breath practitioner. *Breathe better, Sleep Better* offers beautiful insights about *prana* in a fun and accessible manner. An important book illuminating an essential yogic tool."

—Yogrishi Vishvketu, director and founder of World Conscious Yoga Family, teacher of yoga teachers, and author of *Yogasana*

"*Breathe Better, Sleep Better* is an exceptional book that offers a detailed look at how our breath has the ability to be a guiding light in our life. It's an excellent addition to yoga teacher trainings and reader-friendly for beginner students as well. Anandi's expertise in sleep management gives a much-needed look at how the breath is integral in our overall health in body and mind."

—Brenda Feuerstein, PhD, director of Traditional Yoga Studies and co-author of *The Bhagavad-Gita: A New Translation, The Matrix of Yoga, Green Yoga* and *Green Dharma* with Georg Feuerstein, and author of *The Yoga-Sutra from a Woman's Perspective*

"Anandi-ji knows her stuff. Not only will these techniques resolve many sleep issues, but they will also help to strengthen all your organs, tissues, and physical systems. Energetically, your entire being will pulse with radiance, and your mind will become restful. But it requires practice, practice, and more practice. Trust Anandi-ji; surrender your breath and enjoy the results of a peaceful body and mind!"

—Yogi Uday, dedicated yogi and author of
Yogi Yum Yums and *The Mind Is the Trip*

"Overscheduled and busy Executives will relate to the challenge of switching off! '*Breathe Better, Sleep Better*, will of course help you to decompress and recharge through better sleep, but also, the breathing techniques have helped me and my clients prepare for deeper more emotionally intelligent discussions"

—Andro Donovan, Executive coach and author of *Motivate Yourself*

"I'm thrilled to have my poem, Breath is Life's Teacher, include in this wonderful book Anandi has written. Her teaching is grounded in well researched expertise and expressed from such a heart centred place. When you're reading it, you feel as though Anandi is speaking to you personally. I'm sure this book will be a healing gift to everyone who reads it, and especially to anyone suffereing from sleep issues. It is superbly informative and practical, and most of all, inspiring. Congratulations and thank you Anandi"

—Donna Martin, Yoga teacher, body centered psychotherapist,
International Hakomi trainer, creator of Psoma Yoga ™ therapy
and author of *The Breath Poem, Remembering Wholeness, Simply
Being, Seeing your life through new eyes, Embodied Mindfulness:
The Hakomi Way, and The Practice of Loving Presence.*

Foreword

Everything looks better after a good night's sleep. This adage has proven so true for me. Through the hormonal changes of pregnancy and midlife and the persistent sleep disruption of child-rearing, I have noticed firsthand the havoc that is wreaked on the body and mind from poor sleep or sheer sleeplessness. After years of co-sleeping and breastfeeding two children, I found that, even after they finally started sleeping through the night, I woke regularly at one, three, and five in the morning. My body had become used to routine waking during the night. I would wake and groggily pat the bed beside me to see if the baby was okay, wondering why she had not woken to nurse. I often stayed awake through the wee hours of the night, perhaps subconsciously just waiting for the next illusory feeding.

Don't get me wrong. I am so glad I had the rich experience of bonding with the babies in the quiet of night, sharing a bed while rolling over intuitively for them to latch on while we both lay snug and cozy. My difficulties arose more from not being able to flip the switch and go back to deep, continuous sleep after the night waking was no longer called for. Like many people, I needed rebalancing. I needed tools.

For various reasons, we may simply resign ourselves to the reality of poor sleep without addressing it as an issue. After all we may say everybody has a bad night from time to time. But before we know it, poor sleep may be more the norm than the exception. And since the invention of the light bulb and the backlit computer screen, it is true that almost everyone suffers to some degree from a disrupted circadian rhythm. We no longer hunker down for the evening after sunset or enjoy the natural soporific of pitch-black darkness at night. Street lights and light pollution from various sources invade our bedrooms unless we specifically invest in blackout drapes. In addition there is the constant buzz of electrical equipment. And so, too true, we notice that many around us complain of poor sleep or tiredness on waking. But this doesn't mean it is natural or we can't take steps to move towards restoring our bodies' natural rhythms and getting the restorative, rejuvenative sleep our bodies need.

So when Anandi first mentioned to me that she was working on a book on breathing for insomnia, I had an immediate sense that the project would bring effective tools and hope to many. I believe intentionally directing practice to a specific area of our lives for healing and balance gives focus to the practice and awareness of its effect on the quality of our lives. In this way we can tweak and adjust our efforts as necessary, and we become more responsible for and to our practice.

Though this is a book that really hones in on yoga for anxiety and insomnia, *Breathe Better, Sleep Better* offers a perfect blend of theory and practice. Anandi outlines the *vayus*, or different directional flows of breath within the body, the understanding of which was the result of the experimentation and intuition of the early yogis. She uses the map of the *vayus* as a backdrop to explore various needs and deficiencies we may experience and offers insights and techniques to bring balance in various areas. For example, *samana*, the air that circulates in the abdominal region, can be fortified in order to improve digestion and therefore prevent the churning and agitation that so often prevents us from dropping into a restful sleep.

Seasoned practitioners as well as those new to yoga will find both practical wisdom, which is unfortunately not often taught in regular *asana* classes, and inspiration to journey profoundly into the subtle realms of breath work and self-observation and towards nurturance, insight, and greater wellness.

Chétana Jessica Torrens

Acknowledgements

I am eternally grateful to Massimiliano, who very patiently and with love put up with my ongoing breath experiments. None of this would be possible without my family who support me in everything I do, and thank you to Jacqui Malpass, who supported me on this journey!

Chapter 1

The Breath Is Your Sleep Guru

Observe me, says the breath, and learn to live effortlessly in the present moment.
Feel me, says the breath, and feel the ebb and flow of life.
Allow me, says the breath, and I'll sustain and nourish you, filling you with
energy and cleansing you of tension and fatigue.

Move with me, says the breath, and I'll invite your soul to dance.
Make sounds with me and I shall teach your soul to sing.
Follow me, says the breath, and I'll lead you out to the farthest reaches of
the universe, and inward to the deepest parts of your inner world.

Notice, says the breath, that I am as valuable to you coming or going… that
every part of my cycle is as necessary as another… that after I'm released,
I return again and again… that even after a long pause – moments when
nothing seems to happen – eventually I am there.

Each time I come, says the breath, I am a gift from life. And yet you release
me without regret… without suffering… without fear.

Notice how you take me in, invites the breath. Is it with joy… with
gratitude…? Do you take me in fully… invite me into all the inner spaces

of your home? …Or carefully into just inside the door? What places in you am I not allowed to nourish?

And notice, says the breath, how you release me. Do you hold me prisoner in closed up places in the body? Is my release resisted… do you let me go reluctantly, or easily?

And are my waves of breath, of life, as gentle as a quiet sea, softly smoothing sandy stretches of yourself….Or anxious, urgent, choppy waves…Or the crashing tumult of a stormy sea…?

And can you feel me as the link between your inner and outer worlds… feel me as life's exchange between the Universe and You? The Universe breathes me into You… You send me back to the Universe. I am the flow of life between every single part and the whole.

Your attitude to me, says the breath, is your attitude to Life. Welcome me… embrace me fully. Let me nourish you completely, then set me free. Move with me, dance with me, sing with me, sigh with me… Love me. Trust me. Don't try to control me.

I am the breath.
Life is the musician.
You are the flute.
And music –
creativity – depends on all of us. You are not the creator… nor the creation. We are all a part of the process of creativity… You, life, and me: the breath.

—The Breath is Life's Teacher, Donna Martin

The book you are about to read is the result of a twenty-five-year journey into health and well-being. It is the outcome of a search for something that could soothe and heal the trials and tribulations of insomniacs like me and, very probably, you. I discovered the breath takes us from the dungeon of sleeplessness to the heavenly experience of sleeping well. I hope and pray that this book saves you the trouble of searching for many years, as I did, to find a solution. By following the processes I have set out, you will be able to get on the road to recovery a lot sooner.

In the West, little attention seems to be paid to the power of the breath. Even during physical education at school, I never remember anyone teaching me about breathing. Sport was all about winning the game, never about health and inner peace. In the East, however, it is a completely different story, one that goes back in time to an ancient Indian scripture called the *Rig Veda* and beyond. India's love affair with the breath continued with the famous epic *Ramayana*, where the charming monkey god Hanuman symbolises breath. Light as a feather, he moves swiftly and is able to fill expansive and minute spaces alike. He epitomises the profound power of love and is ready to serve humanity with all his strength and creativity. As we become more connected to the breath, we experience Hanuman's qualities of groundedness, clarity, and courage.

According to the Indian wisdom tradition, the breath is a tangible aspect of the spirit that puts us immediately in touch with the divine. The moment we start focusing on the breath, the inner gates of our being start to open. If you look up the Latin word *spiritus*, you will see that it means breath, breathing, inspiration, light breeze, spirit, and energy. The breath, therefore, is indeed worth the exploration.

The health benefits of using the breath are also of interest to allopathic medical institutes in India today. Research is being done to prove that working with the breath reduces the physical manifestation of stress and anxiety. As an example, the department of physiology at the Jawaharlal Institute of Postgraduate Medical Education and Research in India[2] concluded that "regular practice of slow breathing exercises for a minimum of three months improves the autonomic functions. The autonomic nervous system governs the sympathetic (fight or flight) and parasympathetic (rest and restore) responses."

The Insidious Creep of Insomnia

Aged twenty-seven and heading for divorce, I was suffering from severe insomnia. It had crept silently up on me over the previous couple of years and continued to impact me for the next fifteen. Looking back, I clearly did not have the tools to deal with my emotions in those days. And I was mentally drained with a terrible sleep issue. I would toss and turn through long, hard nights, often with no sleep at all, and then collapse in a heap, still unable to sleep.

By the time I hit my mid-thirties, I'd married again and was running my own business teaching to the beauty industry. I had a punishing travel schedule, often getting up at four thirty and driving for three hours before the working day even started. One particular morning, as I clung on to that steering wheel, I wept and wept. I was exhausted. The thought of having to paint a smile on my face and perform as expected filled me with dread. I just wanted to run away from everything and everybody. I could not bear the thought of facing anyone.

As time went on, the stress of my business and the growing strain on my second marriage were starting to show. I lost weight; my insomnia imprisoned me. As each night loomed up, it brought the fear of sleeplessness with it. When we fast-forward a few more years, the effects of sleep deprivation had taken a severe toll on my health. I was in the vicious cycle of the lack of sleep increasing my anxiety levels, making my insomnia even worse. My mouth started to fill with ulcers, my digestion hit an all-time low, and I developed terrible acne rosacea. But that was not all. Bankruptcy was on the horizon, and my second marriage was becoming increasingly fraught and difficult. Despite the state of my health, I was determined not to reach for sleeping pills even though my mother kept offering me some of hers. Eventually I relented and tried one, but I felt even worse the next day. Sleeping pills were definitely not a solution for me.

After a long journey through the world of un-wellness, I was eventually introduced to yoga. Although initially I was only initiated into posture, my dear Guru-ji Yogi Vishvketu later introduced me to working with the breath at a workshop in India. I never looked back. Finally using the breath, I was able to develop the tools to pull myself out of the quagmire of anxiety and insomnia.

It took a while for the penny to drop. I practiced yoga postures for five years before I realised that something was still missing. At last I found that the breath was my teacher, not the obsession I developed for getting myself into even more challenging yoga poses. I found that recovering from sleep deprivation and insomnia was a much more challenging matter than the famous lotus pose.

Life now is very different. I maintain my balance using the techniques you will find in this book. I enjoy and appreciate so much the feeling of being inspired when I wake up in the morning instead of dragging myself through the day, wondering if I will actually make it to nightfall. My message to you is that, by using the power of the breath, you too can rediscover a normal sleeping pattern and live life with joy and enthusiasm.

How Do I Use This Book?

"In the breath, the soul finds an opportunity to speak"

—Donna Faulds

Until now, you may not have realised that the breath impacts everything you do, especially sleep. Within your breath is the story of who you are. By really paying attention to it, you can find both what is out of balance and what you need to do about it. Eventually you will have to listen to the breath's voice.

Have you ever noticed, when you run around going about your day, your mind is racing and your breath becomes shorter? Perhaps when you get stressed multitasking as you zoom among applications on your computer, you realise you are holding your breath. It is as if holding your breath could help you keep it all together. Yes, stress is the enemy of the breath. In these situations, your breath is trying to tell you, "You need to slow down." In this book, I hope to share the rejuvenating power of the breath and show you how it can invigorate your body, mind, and spirit and give you a great night's sleep.

It is important to bear in mind that this is not an intellectual process, just as breathing is not something you usually do consciously. By surrendering to and focusing on the breath, we experience a deep, profound, and nourishing power that we would otherwise spend our entire lives unaware of. The secret energy of the breath is something we need to participate in physically. We need to relearn how to surrender to the natural deep breathing patterns by learning how to relax and let go of insidious tension in the respiratory muscles. As you work through this book, I will be asking you to write down answers to questions and make observations. So please get yourself a journal or notebook that you can dedicate to this journey.

It is important to take your time in reading and contemplating the ideas in this book and to try out the exercises. The only way to understand these concepts is through feeling and experimenting. It is not possible to gain the benefits of the exercises just by reading. They must be experienced.

First I will be taking you through the anatomy of the breath to get you acquainted with your breathing apparatus. This will help you understand that we are doing the exercises in order to free up the breathing muscles of your body. I will show you how to get in touch with the subtler energetic value of the life force in the breath (*prana*) that yoga talks about and guide you through the fascinating journey of the five aspects of the subtle breath, the five *vayus*. Getting to know how these forces work will help you understand the importance of breathing freely and deeply and how this can get you back into balance and sleeping well.

Once you have worked through the various exercises in each of the five *vayus*, I will take you into the Surrendered Breath practice, which brings all the teachings from the previous chapters together, so it is important to work on the exercises in order rather than jumping ahead, at least in the beginning.

I have created a five-week plan to help give structure to your new practice, together with a number of practice recipes for various times when you need help with something in particular.

Sleep Is the Lock, and Breath Is the Key

> *"Modern medicine is just too damn effective"*
>
> —Gandhi

Healing the natural way for a condition like insomnia is not instantaneous like popping a pill, but the benefits far outweigh the pharmaceutical route. You only have to read the instructions inside the medication to find a long list of undesirable and damaging side effects. Tablets might get you to sleep, but the quality will probably be poor, and you are likely to gain another set of problems related to the side effects. As Gandhi so rightly said, "Modern medicine is just too damn effective."

As a society, we are used to quick fixes. It can be difficult to be patient. The only side effects one has with the natural solution to insomnia will include better sleep and more energy. Your digestion may also improve, and you may even find yourself reacting less emotionally when under stress, just to name a few benefits.

If we are to be healthy, life requires balance between rest and movement. This is also true in nature where the energy of the sun brings daytime activity, and as the sun sets, nature becomes quiet as it rests and recuperates, preparing for the next day. If you are on the go from six in the morning and continue to stare at your computer screen until ten in the evening, like most of us are, your brain will not easily switch off. As a result, your physical body will lose its equilibrium and, more than likely, interrupt your natural sleep rhythm.

In ancient times when there were no computers and less pressure to have it all, I imagine that insomnia and sleep deprivation were uncommon. It would benefit us all to bring back a bit more of a balanced approach to work and life goals and allow ourselves time to be human beings, not always human doings. Sleep is one of the natural, automatic responses of the body and mind, and not having enough of it is likely to result in illness to some degree.

If you suffer from stress and insomnia, I urge you to take the time and make the effort to do the exercises I recommend in the later chapters in this book. Good health and better sleep is most certainly within your reach if you do. Before we move on, some of the benefits that can arise from of good breathing are

- better sleep
- general mental and emotional well-being
- a better immune system
- the feeling of being grounded and calm during stress
- a more efficient detoxifying system
- a feeling of being more connected to your spiritual nature
- better concentration
- a calmer mind
- lower blood pressure
- more equilibrium between the parasympathetic and sympathetic nervous systems
- fewer headaches
- the ability of the body to be more efficient at releasing tension in muscles and internal organs.

If you are ready and willing, I look forward to being your guide on this adventure through the mysteries of the breath. Remember: read slowly, participate, and enjoy!

Chapter 2

The Anatomy of the Breath

"Freedom is strangely ephemeral. It is something like breathing; one only becomes acutely aware of its importance when one is choking"

—William Simon

Breathing is an experiential activity, and it is important to feel how the breath moves the body on a practical level. Before you can begin to understand the concepts in this book, it is useful to gain a fuller understanding of how your breathing apparatus works. In this chapter, we will explore the journey of the breath from the nose to the lungs and out again and how the body changes shape to accommodate the breath.

The average person breathes 21,600 times per day, breathing in a combination of 78.04 per cent nitrogen, 21 per cent oxygen, and 0.96 per cent argon and other gases and then breathing out 78.4 per cent nitrogen, 13–16 per cent oxygen, 4–5.3 per cent carbon dioxide, and 1 per cent argon and other gases.[1] Each breath in and out is approximately a half-litre of air.

Let's start at the point where the breath enters your body. Your nose is fitted with an ingenious filtering system to protect your very delicate lungs. It is lined with tiny hairs called cilia that filter inhaled dust and germs to prevent them from entering your lungs. The lining of the nose remains moist, which conveniently leaves a tacky surface attracting bacteria. Another clever invention of Mother Nature is your very own nasal cavity heater. The blood supply to the nasal membranes warms the temperature of the air entering the lungs.

As the breath continues its journey into the lungs, the windpipe divides into two bronchial tubes that split like branches of a tree into thousands of even smaller tubes (bronchioles) that connect to minute sacs called "alveoli." There are approximately 600 million alveoli in our lungs, and this is where all the exciting stuff happens. An incredible symbiotic process of giving and receiving takes place. The in-breath brings in the life force oxygen that is absorbed into the rivers and streams of the body. Your heart then pumps it to every cell of your body. As the in-breath flows seamlessly into the out-breath, metabolic waste gases are carried up through your lungs and out of your mouth and nose. The unconscious activity of the body is an astonishing continuous course of synchronous events.

The Muscles of Respiration

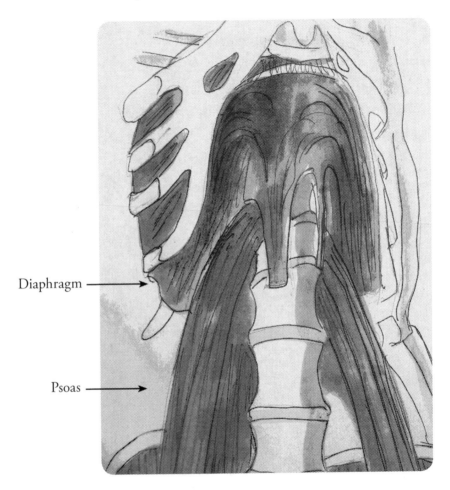

Diaphragm

Psoas

The process of inhaling and exhaling is very complex and involves an immaculately coordinated set of contractions from lots of different muscles. The primary muscle of respiration is, of course, the diaphragm, but accessory muscles assist during the act of breathing too. From the top of the rib cage all the way to the bottom, you have a series of muscles that are layered, angled, and attached in such a way that, once they contract, they pull the rib cage upwards, lifting and opening the chest cavity. The diaphragm is the power behind the breath, and the accessory muscles create the space for the breath.

The inhaling muscles, as we have seen, are the diaphragm and external intercostal muscles. The exhaling muscles are the internal intercostal muscles and the abdominal muscles, the importance of which is often overlooked. Have you ever noticed that you use your abdominal muscles when talking, singing, coughing, or playing a wind instrument? Your internal intercostals alone would not have the power to drive the force required to do any of these activities.

The Depression Muscle

In Kaminoff's *Yoga Anatomy* book, he explains that, when you breathe, the muscles around the skull, neck, and scapulae (shoulder blades) need to be stabilised so the external intercostal muscles can get enough leverage to lift the rib cage. People with dysfunctional breathing often have their shoulders "round their ears" as they try to unconsciously stabilise the skull, neck, and scapulae so the external intercostal muscles can get the leverage they need to contract and lift the thoracic cavity so they can breathe.

When people are under stress, the neck and shoulder muscles get tight, which affects the breathing muscles. Good breathing is all about creating space and shape change, and if the rib cage movement is restricted, the diaphragm will also be restricted.

The transversus thoracis, sometimes known as the depression muscle, is used in exhaling and often becomes tense and short once a person is under stress. This makes inhaling more difficult as the muscles need to work harder to open the thoracic cavity. When these muscles get tight, people become round-shouldered, thinking the resulting backache has something to do with their spine when actually it has more to do with their breathing. They simply need to open and stretch the tight muscles of respiration, and their back problem will disappear.

The Psoas Muscle

The psoas muscle is the major muscle in the body that keeps you upright and balanced. It is closely connected to your sympathetic nervous system and tightens when you are under stress. Liz Koch, in *The Psoas Book*, explains that one of the biggest fears of the human being is the fear of falling. The moment the fight-or-flight response is triggered, one of the consequences is that the psoas muscle tenses in order to stabilise the body. She also goes on to say that, once the psoas shortens and lacks vitality and moisture, it continually triggers the sense of anxiety and fear.

You will see from the diagram above that the psoas and diaphragm are interconnected. The attachments of the diaphragm literally run over the psoas muscle. An exhausted psoas will influence the breath and may leave you finding deep breathing difficult.

Breathing Muscles and Making Space for the Breath

The breath magically happens if we get out of its way! In order to breathe properly, we need to create space and facilitate shape change in the thoracic cavity. It is not the diaphragm alone that creates space. The muscles in the chest need to relax; therefore attempting to exercise the diaphragm on its own is not at all helpful. The diaphragm is only as good as the chest's capacity for shape change.

Some therapists or teachers recommend putting a sandbag on the belly and suggest that you should perform belly breathing. This only exercises the exhaling muscles, which actually pulls down your rib cage and limits the space in the chest. If you try to take deep breaths with a very tight chest, the air has nowhere to go, and deep breathing becomes impossible. To improve the capacity for deep, profound breathing, it will be important to work at opening the chest and making space first.

Understanding the Pause between the In-Breath and Out-Breath

As you start working with the breath, you will gradually become more aware of the pause between the in-breath and out-breath. This will be especially important for the Surrendered Breath practices in chapter 11. The Sanskrit name for this pause is *kumbhaka*, which means "pot like." It is also translated as "breath control." In many spiritual traditions, breath retention is regarded as a fundamental tool to bring the mind to the blissful state of meditation.

As you will see from Umberto Pelizzari, an Italian free diver, something miraculous starts to happen once you are able to hold your breath for long periods of time.

"From the depth of 0 to 100 metres and even deeper, headlong into the abyss, the heart beat gets slower, the body disappears, and all the feelings take a new form. The only thing that remains is the soul. A long jump into the soul, which seems to absorb in the universe. Every time I re-ascend is making a choice: it's me who re-finds myself in my human dimension, metre by metre, to come up, then to see the light again ... In the abyss I look for myself. This is a mystical experience bordering the divine."

If you read many of the ancient texts, you will also see that a long list of magical powers is associated with practicing *kumbhaka*. Achieving magical powers are not our goal in this book, but opening the door to peace and tranquility is.

Once you breathe in a way that is completely relaxed, this pause will naturally become longer. You don't need to do anything apart from surrender and relax. The slightly extended pause due to the state of surrendering and relaxing the body to the earth gives it more time to assimilate oxygen and *prana* (life force energy) and for the exchange of oxygen and carbon dioxide to take place. Short, rushed breath, therefore, gives the body little time to absorb precious oxygen and *prana* and rid itself of carbon dioxide. In the Surrendered Breath practice, you will learn how to use this pause to nourish and detoxify your system.

Chapter 3

The Subtle Breath

"Let life and Prana lift you to a place you've never visited before"

—Danna Faulds

Vital Life Force, *Prana*

You may have thought that breath is just breath, but there is actually a whole world of subtlety in the breath. I am referring to a vital life force that rides with the breath and not something that just keeps us upright. What is the difference between someone who is animated, positive, and joyful and someone who is lethargic, feels down, and moves very little? They will both be breathing, but the latter person more than likely will be breathing in a very limited way, which means that, apart from the oxygen levels, they don't have the same amount of subtle energy.

The subtle energy gives you the oomph to go about your day with energy and joy. This supercharged esoteric energy source is called *prana*, and the *pranic* aspect of the breath is called *vayu*. *Prana* gives you energy, enthusiasm, and a true sense of being alive. We will later explore *vayu*, but there are a number of other possibilities for *pranic* expansion, which I will share with you briefly.

Prana Source: Food

> *"Let thy food be thy medicine"*
>
> —Hippocrates

Food is a fundamental source of *prana* from which we create our physical being. Not only does your body need food for growth, repair, and energy, it will reflect whatever you put into it. A diet rich in live, organic, and nutritious foods will play a very important part in your vitality. Good food can make you feel invigorated and truly alive. Heavily processed food, on the other hand, will make you feel dull, lethargic, and uninspired.

Prana Source: Trees

> *"I took a walk in the woods and came out taller than the trees"*
>
> —Henry Thoreau

Trees touch our lives and play such an important part in keeping our world in balance, yet many take them for granted. We excessively destroy rain forests as we try to farm, dig for oil, and build dams. Not only do trees give homes to all sorts of animals, they provide us with raw materials for medicines, help regulate the climate, and prevent soil erosion. They are, of course, also busily consuming our exhaled carbon dioxide and giving us life in the form of oxygen. Each human being needs the oxygen supply from roughly seven or eight trees to survive per year. It's a shame that we, particularly in the West, have not quite grasped the fact that the act of destroying trees is intrinsically connected to diminishing our very own life force.

Mike McAliney, in *Arguments for Land Conservation: Documentation and Information Sources for Land Resources Protection*, states that a single mature tree can absorb carbon dioxide at a rate of forty-eight pounds per year and release enough oxygen back into the atmosphere to support two human beings.

Prana Source: Contact with the Earth

"I only went out for a walk, and finally concluded to stay out till sundown, for going out, I found, was really going in"

—John Muir

Most of us don't even touch the ground with bare feet, but if we put our feet on the surface of Mother Earth, she will give us a charge of energy that will make us look, feel, and sleep better. There is some very interesting research published in the *Journal of Environmental and Public Health*[4] on how direct physical contact with the electrons on the surface of the earth can have a positive effect on our health.

They took two groups of people and gave them earthing sheet (a sheet connected to the main earth connection) to sleep on. Twenty-three out of twenty-seven participants reported an overall 85 per cent improvement in the time it to took fall asleep. Twenty-five out of the twenty-seven reported a 93 per cent improvement in the quality of their sleep. And twenty-one out of the twenty-seven reported a general improvement in the sense of well-being.

Just having your feet in contact with the earth for thirty minutes, you will notice that stress dissipates, breathing becomes deeper, and you will feel more energised. In our modern-day life, maintaining contact with the earth becomes extremely challenging, especially for those who live in apartments nestled in the midst of busy city life. Remember to get out in nature often. It truly feeds your soul.

Prana Source: Connection to Your Higher Self

> *"You can think of your body in two ways: one, as mechanical, like an automobile worth only so many miles or as a living breathing energetic vessel manifested from spirit. Either way will greatly affect the length and quality of your life. Choose wisely"*
>
> —Gary Hopkins

Being connected to your higher self expands *prana*. Feeling inspired and connected to your purpose is hugely nourishing. You may not have realised it, but being bored diminishes your life force and makes you feel lethargic and uncreative. Deep breathing exercises will refresh the brain and get you reconnected to your inner wisdom by quietening the constant chatter in the mind and giving you mental space.

Prana Source: Be Around Positive People

Surround yourself with only people who are going to lift you higher. Life force will always try to shine the light and transform the darkness. Spend as much time as possible with lighter energy and people who encourage the highest in you.

Prana Source: Home Environment

Your home environment should be a sanctuary and a restorative space where you can recharge and feel nourished. Accumulated clutter will drag you and your energy down. Make your home a sacred environment that welcomes you as soon as you walk in the door.

Prana Source: Sunlight

> "*Sunlight fell upon the wall; the wall received a borrowed splendor. Why set your heart on a piece of earth, O simple one? Seek out the source which shines forever*"

> —Rumi

We all dash out to buy the latest sunscreen, but remember that the sun boosts the immune system, soothes depression, heals wounds, and makes you feel great, to name a few benefits. The sunlight is one of the most powerful sources of *prana*. Without the sunlight, there would be no life on earth. Don't be scared of the sun and avoid it completely. Just choose your time wisely to get connected to the solar aspect of *prana*.

Exercise: What Is Your *Prana* Score?

Score your *prana* levels from zero as very poor to five as well stocked up.

Food and diet	
Being out in nature	
Contact with the earth	
Connection with your higher self	
Company you keep	
Home environment	
Sunlight	

Now write in your journal one thing that you could do on each item to improve your score.

The Energetic Rivers of the Body

According to Eastern philosophy, a whole network of *pranic* energy channels called *nadis* pervade the body. The word *nadi* in Sanskrit means "flow," "motion," or "vibration." Think of this energy flowing through you like a river that is always moving and vibrating. The Tantric yogis said there are seventy-two thousand of these freely trickling *pranic* energy brooks, busy streams, and flowing majestic rivers meshed around your body. Although medical science and microscopes can't detect them, anyone working in the field of healing and energy work. For example, Qi Gong, Reiki, and vibrational medicine can sense the subtle energy in the body. Dr. Carl Jung also took a great interest in the subject, which you can see from his book, *The Psychology of Kundalini Yoga*. Obstructed, congested energy channels contribute to the lack of well-being we experience in the West. The sooner we start to become conscious of the *pranic* rivers, the better.

There are three principal *nadis* of great interest. The most noble of these is the *Sushumna*, which runs through the centre of the body from the base of the spine to the top of the head. The psycho-spiritual energy, known in the yoga world as *Kundalini Shakti*, when awakened, thunders up the *Sushumna* with the force of the raging river Ganges in monsoon.

The other significant *nadis* are the two running on either side of this channel from the root of the body to the point between the eyebrows. The one on the left is called *Ida*; the one on the right is called *Pingala*. These two *nadis* spiral around the *Sushumna*, crossing over at specific points called *chakras*, a vortex of energy relating to different levels of consciousness. Think of it as something that spins like a wheel and opens like a flower.

Your Two Halves

The left side of your brain controls the right side of your body; the right side of your brain controls the left side of your body. The right side of the body, the left side of the brain, is seen as the core of masculine qualities such as logic and reason. It is also related to the sun's solar energy and the sympathetic nervous system. The left side of the body, the right side of the brain, is considered the core of feminine qualities like intuition, creativity, and spontaneity. The left side relates to the cooling lunar energy and the parasympathetic nervous system.

Your breathing is closely connected to the natural shifts between these two sides of your brain. Did you ever notice that one side of the nostril is always more open than the other? In a healthy person, this shifts about every one and a half to two hours. When digesting food, for example, the body needs solar, digestive energy, and your right nostril will be more open. Once you are more relaxed or need cooling energy, for example, in very hot weather, your left nostril will be more open. If you lie on your right side when trying to sleep, your left nostril will become freer. As the left nostril is connected to quiet lunar energy, it will help you unwind, relax, and go to sleep.

By working with a breathing exercise called *Anuloma Viloma*—or alternate nostril breathing—you can start restoring and reintegrating the solar and lunar energy forces and bring balance and equilibrium back to your system.

On a physical level, alternate nostril breathing has some marvelous health benefits. For example, you will be bringing more oxygen supplies into the body and purifying the blood. On a mental level, it will calm those out-of-control emotions and release bouts of stress. Greater equilibrium can also boost your immune system, and you are also likely to find that your sleep patterns starts to improve.

Exercise: *Anuloma Viloma*

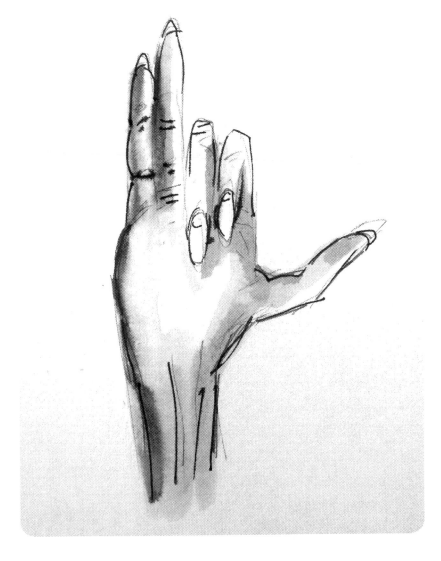

Get yourself into a comfortable position, sitting up straight. You can be in a chair or sitting on a cushion on the floor. The key is to keep your back straight but not rigid. Think energy channels! Slumped spines mean blocked rivers and stagnant water. So keep that back upright.

Now you need to organise your right hand in a special position called *Vishnu Mudra*, which is used in particular for this breathing technique. Ready? Raise your right hand. Leave your thumb and ring and little finger open. Keep the first and second fingers bent towards the palm of the hand.

Take in a long, deep breath. Then exhale and close your right nostril with your right thumb. Inhale through the left nostril. Close your left nostril with your ring finger, and exhale through the right nostril. Inhale through the right nostril, keeping your left nostril closed. Close the right nostril with your thumb, and exhale through the left nostril. This is one full round.

Start by doing eleven rounds of simple *Anuloma Viloma,* or as instructed in the practice guides in the following chapters. Make the inhale as long and deep as possible, and exhale until you are empty without straining.

Warning: *Anuloma Viloma* can be developed further, but I recommend you start with this simple version and consult a teacher if you wish to move on to more advanced *pranayama*.

Finding Equilibrium When We Need It

It is possible to tap into the power of *Ida*, the lunar feminine energy, and *Pingala*, the solar masculine energy, when we need their influence in our daily lives. If we focus on breathing through the left nostril, we would be creating a calming and releasing breath. Conversely, if we focused on breathing through the right nostril, this would have an energising, more stimulating effect.

Exercise: *Surya Bedhi*

Draw on the energetic warm energy of the sun, the morning side. Try this ten-minute morning *pranic* energy boost. Get yourself in a comfortable position, sitting up straight. You can be in a chair or sitting on a cushion on the floor. Organise your right hand into *Vishnu Mudra*. Close your left nostril with your right ring finger, and inhale through your right nostril. Close your right nostril with your right thumb, and exhale through your left. This is one round. Make your in-breath as long and as deep as possible and your out-breath slow and complete.

Start by doing eleven rounds of *Surya Bedhi*, or as instructed in the practice guides in the following chapters. Make the inhale as long and deep as possible, and exhale until you are empty without straining.

Exercise: *Chandra Bedhi*

Invite in the calming, soothing lunar energy, the evening side. This is your ten-minute evening nourishment and sleep aid. Get into your chosen position of comfort. Remember your straight spine. Organise your right hand into *Vishnu Mudra*. Close your right nostril with your right thumb. Inhale through the left nostril. Close your left nostril with your right ring finger, and exhale through the right. This is one round. Make your in-breath as long and as deep as possible and your out-breath slow and complete.

Start by doing eleven rounds of *Chandra Bedhi*, or as instructed in the practice guides in the following chapters. Make the inhale as long and deep as possible, and exhale until you are empty without straining.

Introducing *Prana Vayu*

"Undying, untouched by fire or the storms of life, there is a place inside where stillness and abiding peace reside. You can ride the breath to go there"

—Danna Faulds

We have seen that *prana*, although it is not a tangible thing detectable by science, is the vibrational energy force behind all the aspects of your life. Let's say it's the zing and dynamism behind your ability to be active in the world in a positive way. *Prana*, however, is the collective name given to this life-giving essence. *Vayu* is an aspect of *prana* and relates to the breath. The word *vayu* translates as "wind," synonymous with movement. The root of the word *vayu*, or *va*, means "that which flows." So one could describe *vayu* as a force that moves throughout the system. *Prana vayu* actually divides into five internal magical directional forces. You may have been in a yoga class and heard the word *prana*, but these five internal directional forces of *prana* are rarely given the attention they deserve.

Each *vayu* has a physical direction, action, a place in the body, and a psychology as a result of its duties. Once all of these energies are in harmony, you will be oozing health and vitality, yet imbalances in these *pranic* forces will manifest in all sorts of physical and psychological problems. By becoming aware of these different forces, we are able to work at rebalancing the energy force that is depleted or lacking or draw on the individual power of each *vayu* when we need it. Here's a quick peek at what they are:

Prana Vayu	Chapter 4	The "ascending moving air" moves inwards at the same time as it expands the chest. This energy governs everything that comes into your body and provides the driving force in our lives.
Samana Vayu	Chapter 5	The "balancing air" moves from the periphery of the body to the centre. This energy processes and digests on all levels.
Vyana Vayu	Chapter 6	The "outward moving air" moves from the centre outwards. This energy keeps everything moving, including emotions and thoughts.
Apana Vayu	Chapter 7	The "air that moves away" moves downwards and out. It allows you to let go of the negative and toxic.
Udana Vayu	Chapter 8	The "upward moving energy" moves upwards and is the creative force that allows you to express yourself in the world.

Chapter 4

The Magic of Prana Vayu

If you've woken up breathing, you have another chance to live your dreams.

It was tremendously exciting to become aware of the possibilities of working with the breath, and I got very excited, especially when I started feeling a new type of vitality in my body. As subtle transformations slowly started to happen, I realised the *prana* was to be my alchemist.

First, silent and as yet unexplored elements of my being started to spring into life. They were subtle, none of that crash, bang, and wallop stuff that my years as a high-impact aerobics instructor gave me. I started to feel calm yet more energised than ever, but in mindful ways.

I found myself one day at the top of our local mountain, staring across the valley. It had rained the night before and surrounded me with fresh sweet *prana* and dew at my feet. As I took in the sights of the emerging day, I suddenly noticed that I wasn't out of breath or excited, just calm, connected, and grounded. I then realised how wonderful it was to just breathe fresh *pranic* air. To breathe and not be thinking about everyday life and the turmoil whirling around in my space certainly was refreshing. At that moment, I knew I was on the right path towards achieving my goal of generally being more peaceful and, in particular, getting a good night's sleep.

Once you feel the magic of more *prana* for the first time, don't be surprised if you find yourself seeing the world through new eyes and wondering at things that you don't need to walk up a mountain to discover. Being truly alive will be an altogether new experience.

What I noticed, as will you, is that my thoughts slowed down and I felt more connected to my core and everything around me. All of a sudden, I felt as if I had twiddled the dial on the radio to just the right station, a cosmic radio station, where they are playing just the right songs to get my body grooving and energy flowing.

In a Nutshell: *Prana Vayu*, the Sweet Vital Force of Life

Prana brings air and life force into our bodies, and it is the first step towards greater health and awareness. *Prana* means "air that moves forward," and it is in charge of time. Each day it gently nudges us along towards our dreams and goals. *Prana* is the driving force behind our existence and helps us to give birth to fresh ideas. Imagine it as the new spring season when plants and flowers start to emerge from the darkness of winter and the sunrise. Without *prana*, nothing would move or grow. *Prana* is the vitalising breath, the spark of life that brings the light of the sun with it. As *prana* rises to greet the day, it lights the path and gives us a gentle shove towards going for what we want.

We know the heart is the centre of life-energy circulation, and *prana* resides here. The electrical energy field of our heart is one hundred thousand times stronger and the magnetic field five thousand times stronger than that of our brain, which gives us a clue that this is something more powerful than a mere blood pump. Your heart, the first to form in the womb, is the central point of the body that regulates and balances life.

When you meet someone with lots of *prana*, you feel yourself connecting to a powerful energetic source. You will notice that you feel good around him or her as the symbiotic giving and receiving of energy occurs. We are constantly interacting with the environment and those around us, mostly unconsciously, at a profound spiritual level.

I would now like you to consider your breath in relation to your heart. This may be the first time anyone has asked you to stop and think about the breath and body in a more spiritual way. Right now, try closing your eyes and taking your internal gaze to where your heart is. And imagine you are breathing into your heart instead of your lungs. It may take a bit of practice to keep your attention there, but keep trying. Notice what happens when you focus on your heart. With just a few conscious deep breaths into the heart, you will find that the heart rate decreases and your mind stops running. Note down in your journal anything that comes up, no matter how insignificant it may seem.

Prana is also connected to vision. Shakespeare talks of the eye painting a picture on the heart, which beautifully captures what the eye sees and how it engages with the heart. Try keeping your eyes open and looking at something beautiful. Breathe once more into your heart. What do you notice this time? You may see or feel nothing, or you may start to feel the breath expand and open a connection to something else deep inside of you. We will refer to this place as your soul.

At a basic level, the soul houses our values. It is who we are and what we believe in. You might have heard the phrase, "Selling your soul to the devil." That means doing something that goes across your values, that is, not being true to who you are. Another one is to "bare your soul," where you may share something intimate and special with others. So as you can see, your soul is an intrinsic part of who you are, and we want to get connected to it when working with our breath. Happy souls sleep at night.

As you breathe into your heart, *pranic* vision opens. Think about what you might have as a vision for your life or your dreams. What might be getting in the way? When you have an authentic view of your goals and you take actions to realise them, you will sleep better because you are clearing the clutter, and your life will start to rock. It's like walking into a shop, where everything is beautifully laid out and you can see what you want without having to rummage around. When you look into the eyes of someone with high levels of *prana*, you will notice that the whites of the eyes are beautifully clear. Take a look into your own eyes. What do you see? What about the people around you?

As you think about your vision and dreams, do you feel they are real or hard to reach? *Prana* helps us in the creation of new ideas. Is there something that you would really want to be part of your life, but you are scared to make it a reality? If the answer is yes, please stick to the program laid out in this book because, as you breathe and start bringing in more *prana*, you may start to feel that you are giving birth to something new.

The Role of *Prana*

Just as you and I have roles within our families or businesses, so does *prana*. *Prana* is akin to a project manager whose role is to reduce risk and ensure that all activities run to order with the right resources. These synchronised activities keep the project going and mean that the objectives of the project can be met as expected.

In order to survive, your body also has a whole host of synchronised activities. If you have ever gone onto YouTube and typed in "human cell," you will see an array of videos that demonstrate what an amazing process life is. You will also notice that it is completely organised by something greater than ourselves. Everything in our bodies is part of a system, and we are all systems within the universal system. Every element has a role and function to play. When an element is out of whack, the system starts to fall over.

Within these systems, an order of events and a hierarchy of energies make certain things happen at the right time. Consider how the heart operates. It is divided into two pumps that have to work together. Blood coming back from the organs and tissues enters the right side of your heart, which then pumps it to your lungs. Your lungs remove waste carbon dioxide from the blood and recharge it with oxygen. The oxygenated blood that leaves your lungs enters the left side of your heart, which then pumps it to all parts of your body. It is a system that has a cycle, which works because *prana* is the force that propels everything into action. *Prana* is the spark that ignites and kicks off the cycle.

In each cycle of life, there is birth, decay, and death. In order for things to run smoothly, the organised energy of the *vayus* creates the mysterious life force behind these cycles. *Prana* is the power (our project manager) that gets behind all the other four internal *vayus*. He is the spring season who awakens our fertility and creativity, which, once mixed with universal life force, provides a pathway to new ventures and ways of being.

The following rather endearing tale points out that you cannot survive without *prana* and how your mind is actually quite out of control without it. If you want to take control of your life and health, you have to start with *prana*.

Who Is the King of the Castle?

My version of a story from the Upanishads (an ancient Indian scripture) about Prana

Prana was arguing with the mind and senses about who the supreme was. Along with prana (the breath), there was the mind, speech, ear, and eye. The argument represents the usual human condition of lack of integration where our faculties simply could not agree. So instead of working together as a team, they continued to fight with their ego.

As they could not resolve this issue, prana decided to subtly prove his importance by suggesting each leave the body one at a time to see how the body got on without each. In their ignorance they all agreed, and the experiment began.

First the speech left, but the body did not miss speech much. It did not need it to live. Then the eyes left. Although blind, the body continued. It didn't need eyes either. Next the ears left. Not being able to hear, the body kept going. There was no need for ears to survive. Finally the mind left. Even though unconscious, the body managed to press on. Then prana walked off, but as soon as it started to go, all the other faculties felt their energy draining away and started gasping for prana and pleading with it to come back.

Prana was subsequently voted supreme boss and power within.

The upshot of the story, therefore, is that we need *prana* to function on all levels of our existence. Without this life force, we would not be able to do anything. The mind might think it's in control, but it's totally out of control without *prana*. The breath, in fact, is the most tangible aspect of *prana*, which is why it is of such interest and fascination to the ancient yogis of India.

Mr Prana

We already know that *Mr Prana* is the project manager and a decision-maker. He organises, oversees, and guides life. *Mr Prana* decides what comes into our space, both physically and mentally, and that includes air, liquid, food, and information from all of the senses. He is always full of light. Remember that he is the sunrise. Wherever he goes, he gives life and love, and he is a joy to be around. Because *prana* is connected to the air element, when you breathe into your heart, you meet the energy of *Mr Prana*. *He* can touch everything with the energy of his heart. When he is abundant and flowing, he has an air of greatness about him and demonstrates qualities of strength and courage. *Mr Prana* is deeply connected to his higher self and works through intuition to guide you.

With his intuitive planning, he is your *pranic* guidance system, not dissimilar to a GPS in your car. Of course the GPS will only guide you to the right destination if you tell it where to take you and there is no traffic to slow you down or road works to get in your way. One of the things we often fail to do on long journeys is to give ourselves enough preparation and recovery time. Without these *Mr Prana* can become weak. When he gets tired, he is unable to concentrate and provide leadership to his team. Toxins build up and easily penetrate through the golden gates of the body. Once toxins overload the system, they flood the guidance system with false information. Imagine the human body without a guiding force where the cells do not know what they are supposed to be doing. The result is chaos, a loss of equilibrium, anxiety, and, more than likely, insomnia.

It is difficult to imagine these processes going on inside of us because it is something we take very much for granted until it starts to malfunction of course.

Psychology of *Prana Vayu*

You have seen the potential power of *prana* physically, but getting enough *prana* has profound psychological effects as well. *Prana* is responsible for your ability to take in the positive aspect of your experience and nourishment from the five senses, not just air, food, and drink. It also gives you access to the more meaningful aspects of your thoughts and feelings, and it will give you a clear and focused mind. By taking in enough *prana*, you will be better equipped to deal with negative emotions. *Prana* is like a positive propulsive energy force that motivates you to look for spiritual growth. As you become more connected to *prana*, you become more connected to your higher self. Think of it like being constantly plugged into an abundant cosmic life force. You might even find that you become someone you really like being and actually start enjoying being you. You may also find that you start being a magnet for marvelous opportunities. Remember the heart's electrical force is pulsating and attracting others to you.

When your *pranic* connection is faulty, you may start feeling down, moody, and unwell. You may also notice that you get a lot of headaches and can't think, clearly finding yourself in a rather negative space. You may have overextended yourself and started eating junk food because you simply don't have time to think. In this case, you will start finding yourself making rubbish choices, sliding down that slippery slope to the prison of mediocre health and chronic insomnia. You may find that you are craving an extra glass of wine or even a cigarette. Perhaps you will be running around chasing your tail, taking no time to reconnect to *prana*, the cosmic source of existence. If you don't listen to your intuitive voice tell you to slow down and take stock, your body will soon insist.

Let's Check In

Check your *prana* levels by asking yourself the following questions.

	Yes/ No
Do I feel that I am using my whole lung capacity when I breathe deeply?	
Am I able to spend at least ten minutes per day breathing free, clean air in nature?	
Do I feel present and able to appreciate the blessings I have in this moment?	
Do I always balance my work with my own self-care and nourishing time?	
Do I choose to spend time mostly with the people who inspire and nourish me?	
Do I feel refreshed in the morning?	
Do I see the glass as half-full as opposed to half-empty?	

How did you do? Make a note in your journal of the things you need to work on, and make sure you take action. For example, get yourself out in nature and feel gratitude pulse through your veins. Choose to change your daily routine to include more "me time," or start changing your perspective and seeing your glass as half-full instead of half-empty.

Reflection and *Pranic*-Expanding Goals

Now take some time to reflect. Consider how you can use the wisdom of *Mr Prana* to help you set goals that connect with your heart and get you on your journey to personal and spiritual growth and a good night's sleep.

Purpose	Create a sense of purpose in your life.
Realistic	We know that Rome wasn't built in a day. Be realistic, and give yourself the gift of time.
Align	Everything you do must align to your values. Splitting yourself into lots of pieces that don't represent you will drain your *prana* supply.
Nurturing	Remember to nurture yourself in a nourishing environment. Remember that it expands *prana*.
Accountable	Take responsibility and be accountable for your health and well-being. No one can do this for you. Learn to say no when you absolutely know you need time to resource yourself.

Now Set Your Goals

Write down your goals as if you have already achieved them. Here are some examples to get you started:

- I created a *prana* food menu for this week.
- I organised my time to ensure I had enough personal space.
- I told everyone I am recharging myself this week, and I will not be available for social engagements.

Let's Get More *Prana*

Let me ask you a question. Are you a supercharged magnet for positivity, health, and well-being? Or do you need some help? If your answer is yes, invite more *prana* into your life, physically and psychologically, as I have described below. First read through to the end at least once so you understand it. When you are ready, try the exercises below, and write your reflections in your journal.

Discover the Hidden Gateway of *Prana Vayu*

To prepare us for the practice of the Surrendered Breath later, we need to locate each of the *vayus*. In Orit Sen-Gupta's book, *Vayu's Gate*, she gives us an insight into finding the trigger points of each of the *vayus*, which I will share with you. Let's start with *prana vayu*.

Follow this special *prana vayu* practice. The home of *prana* is the heart, and the trigger point is sternal, at the bottom of the sternum, which is about four fingers above the navel. Find a seated comfortable position with the back straight. Remember: no slumped spines. We want all those energy channels to be open and free to receive *prana*. Now become aware of the breath in the area of the chest, taking deep, long breaths. Bring your awareness to the sternal and imagine you are sending the exhale right into the centre of this point, and keep exhaling and emptying your lungs as much as you can. You may notice that the area around the trigger point becomes more compact. As you inhale, breathe from the point just above the trigger point. By breathing in this way, your chest will expand and rise in all directions simultaneously. Repeat for ten breaths.

See: Visualisation Exercise

You can do this visualisation exercise at any time, and no one will ever know. Do it at home, the supermarket, or even the bus stop. By focusing on channeling the positive energy of *prana* into your body, you will be plugging yourself into the subtle realm of superconscious sprightliness.

Here is the how. Take your focus off any negative emotions, and bring it back to the breath. And take your mind to the *prana vayu* point. As you inhale, imagine a stream of bright light entering your heart, and watch or feel your lungs expand. As you continue to inhale, imagine this energetic light of *prana* gradually filling the whole body. Each time you breathe in, count to eight, and each time you breathe out, count to eight. Repeat for ten breaths.

Feel: Hands Breathing

Hands breathing helps wake up the breathing apparatus by getting the chest moving. It also helps make space for a nice, deep inhale. You are ten breaths away from being able to bounce your way through the next few hours. Sit either on a chair or the floor with your spine up straight. As you inhale, take your hands up above your head as high as you can, and then as you exhale, bring your hands down to either side of your shoulders. Exhale quickly and strongly. Repeat for ten breaths, and on the last breath, inhale the arms up as before. Hold the breath for a moment, and gently bring your hands down with the exhale and rest them on your knees. Do three sets of ten breaths. Notice how much lighter and alive you feel!

Eat: *Prana* Food

Foods rich in *prana* are the lightweight, super nutritious foods full of antioxidants, vitamins, and minerals. Foods that are abundant in the spring and grow quickly are especially high in *prana*. The following are some examples: freshly sprouted seeds, avocado, broccoli, kale, blueberries, chia seeds, and Goji berries.

***Prana* Affirmation**

Our lives are an outer manifestation of our inner thoughts and beliefs. The sooner you start thinking more positively, the sooner your life and environment will start to respond. This is not a new concept. Affirmations have been used for thousands of years. Using appropriate affirmations will expand positive energy in your space. Try this *prana* affirmation: "Vitality grows and glows within every single cell of my body." Sit comfortably, and close your eyes. Repeat the affirmation over and over again for five minutes. Make a note of how you feel in your journal.

Reminder

- Remember that this is our first introduction to Mr Prana and we are working our way through each of the vayus, getting to know each one in turn.
- Take your time and try out all of the exercises as instructed.
- Write down your reflections and thoughts in your journal.
- This is the preparation for the five-week plan.
- You will find video resources for the exercises in this book at www.breathebettersleepbetter.co.uk
- You will find recipes for Prana food at www.breathebettersleepbetter.co.uk

Chapter 5

The Warrior Fire in Your Belly, *Samana Vayu*

"From the unnamed vastness beneath the mind,
I breathe my way to wholeness and healing"

—Danna Faulds

It always fascinates me when anyone talks about his or her insomnia. The focus is usually on how he or she couldn't sleep because of a busy mind. He or she talks about how all of his or her thoughts are being tossed around like clothes in a noisy tumble dryer and how sick and crabby he or she feels the next day, often with no appetite or craving something sweet. If only it were as easy as switching off a light to stop the maelstrom of ramblings whizzing around in our heads.

If this scenario resonates with you, I would like to invite you to consider a disturbed digestive system, which could be the reason for you not being able to sleep. When continually in a state of fight-or-flight, the body pays little attention to the digestive system. It is too busy preparing itself to deal with the stress at hand. All the precious energy required for the digestion process is diverted away from the stomach and intestines.

If your digestion has become slow due to exhaustion and stress, your evening meal is likely to remain in the stomach like a dense brick. If your body is trying to digest a lot of food going into the night, it will disturb the quality of your sleep, for sure. It is always best to eat a light meal in the evening and, if possible, no later than seven.

Let me take you back to the early part of my insomnia. I had no reason to connect sleep deprivation with bad digestion. Like most people, I thought those tumbling thoughts held me captive through torturous nights, one after the other. However, as my insomnia continued, my digestion got worse. I often felt sick and suffered from a lot of bloating and gas. It was a vicious circle. I was not managing my stress levels, which the lack of sleep exacerbated and my digestive problems made even worse. I did not realise that breath had anything to do with digestion in those days, so it never occurred to me to look to my breath as a healing tool.

When I did start working with the breath, in particular consciously focusing on deep diaphragmatic breathing, I noticed I became less reactive to stress, my sleep improved, and my digestion started to become more regular. I had spent years going to the toilet at random times of the day and not always with satisfying results.

Digestion is a complex process. It starts at the mouth and winds its way down your body with your belly at the central point. Your food takes an intriguing journey along a nine-metre nerve-lined pathway. In its simplest form, it is a group of organs that work together to convert food into energy.

However, another side to the gut can't be overlooked. Our gut is often referred to as the "second brain." Professor Michael Ghershon at the Columbia University Medical Centre devoted many years of study in the field of neurogastroenterology and, in 1998, published *The Second Brain*, where you will find all of his research about the connection between our emotions and the gut.

According to Professor Ghershon, the gut has its own nervous system known as the enteric nervous system (ENS), which is central to the operation of the human body and has the capability to function independent of the brain in our head. To me, this system seems to be way too complicated to have evolved only to make sure things move out of the colon.

Our gut or our second brain is not quite wired in the way that our first brain is, but nonetheless it is considered to have an important role not only in our digestion but also on mood. The second brain contains a network of around 100 million neurons, more than in either the spinal cord or peripheral nervous system. To put that into perspective, the brain has around 100 billion neurons. The second brain communicates with the first brain with various messages that affect our mental state. That's a lot of horsepower to look after us, so don't think for one minute that this vast network of neurons only handles our digestion.

Our digestive system, that group of organs with its millions of neurons, grinds its way through a lot of food every day. Maybe it's about time we said "Thank you" for all of its hard work and started to treat it with a little more respect. If you ask any Ayurvedic practitioner, he or she will tell you that our health is hugely dependent on our digestion. That being the case, it is fascinating to see what people actually put into their mouths. What is more, it is shocking that allopathic doctors undervalue the role of diet when treating patients, despite a large and increasing body of literature supporting its importance.

Let's step away from the research and science for a moment and think about some of the things we might say about our guts:

- I've got a gut feeling about such-and-such.
- I can't concentrate because I have butterflies in my tummy.
- I need some fire in my belly.

- I have a sinking feeling in my stomach

When we get these feelings, we react and behave in a certain way. What if we could change the way we behave through breathing and, as a consequence, improve our digestion, quiet our minds, and get to sleep?

The good news is that we can actually change the brain's response by the way that we use our breath. Just by putting a little attention on the breath, it starts to expand and lengthen. The mind settles down and allows the gut to continue the process of digestion more efficiently. This is because our brain is connected to our gut by the vagus nerve, which works with the parasympathetic nervous system, which triggers the relaxation response. So aside from the fact that we need to put good fuel into our body for the digestive system to run on, the quality of the nutrients and the way we breathe plays a key role in our health and disease.

Before we move on to discover *Mrs. Samana*, I would like to ask you to reflect on what you have eaten in the last forty-eight hours. How do you feel, how are your thoughts, how is your digestion, and how have you slept? Just stop for another moment and notice if your breath is shallow or long and deep. How are you feeling right now?

In a Nutshell: *Samana Vayu*, the Intimate Light of Truth

The digestive energy of *samana*, as you may guess, resides in the middle of your body, in the solar plexus, an area between the bottom of the lungs and the navel. It moves from the periphery of the body, discerning and churning its way inwards to the centre through food, air, and thoughts. It is a smooth transition point between the inward and outward forces, digesting life and processing emotions. *Samana* is like a motorway junction, a connection between north, south, east, and west. The ancient yogis saw *samana* as a connection to the sense of sight burning away the fog so you can see things more clearly. *Samana* is the heat of the midday sun in the height of summer. It ripens fruit and transforms vegetables into the digestible food we need for our existence.

Samana is a force to be reckoned with, processing many aspects and elements of our lives (working, eating, drinking, having experiences, and an awful lot of thinking) and, all the while, creating and storing energy. When all of this processing is going on, it creates heat (fire), and heat is energy. Our food contains energy, the air we breathe has energy, and every cell in our body has an energetic impulse. People with balanced *samana* bring passion and energy into everything they do.

Remember: we said that *prana* is the first step to bringing life to our dreams and goals. Unfortunately if *samana* is not working well, you will find yourself lacking in energy and the willpower to enjoy life and bring your dreams and goals to fruition. You will end up tired and feeling old sooner than you think. *Samana* offers us the equilibrium we are all searching for, and that's the fire in our belly!

Now close your eyes, and take your focus to your belly. You might find yourself feeling a little self-conscious and wanting to suck it in. Take a few conscious breaths into your belly. (And yes, let it all hang out.) What happens with your mind chatter? Make a note of what you witness in your journal.

The Role of *Samana*

Samana is the cook and creates the fuel to make everything else happen. Providing *prana* (air, liquid, food, and information from all of the senses) is bringing in the right (good quality) raw materials, *samana* can get on with the job and fire up the rest of the team. *Samana*'s job involves managing the flow of everything from your senses to your food. Food can take between twenty-four and seventy-two hours, depending on the type of food you eat and the efficiency of *samana*.

Let's look at how food flows through your system. The first major muscle movement occurs when food or liquid is swallowed. Although we are able to start swallowing by choice, once the swallow begins, it becomes involuntary and proceeds under the control of the nervous system.

The esophagus is the organ into which the swallowed food is pushed. It connects the throat above with the stomach below. At the junction of the esophagus and stomach, a ringlike valve (sphincter) closes the passage between the two organs. However, as the food approaches the closed ring, the surrounding muscles relax and allow the food to pass.

The food then enters the stomach, which has three mechanical tasks to do:

1. The stomach must store the swallowed food and liquid, requiring the muscle of the upper part of the stomach to relax and accept large volumes of swallowed material.
2. Next is to mix up the food, liquid, and digestive juices produced by the stomach. The lower part of the stomach mixes these materials by its muscle action.
3. Finally the stomach empties its contents slowly into the small intestine.

Several factors affect the emptying of the stomach, including the nature of the food, the degree of muscle action of the emptying stomach, and the ability of *samana* to maintain the energy to do this. As the food is digested in the small intestine and dissolved into the juices from the pancreas, liver, and intestine, the contents of the intestine are mixed and pushed forward to allow further digestion. This whole process takes an awful lot of energy, which is why you often feel like sleeping after a heavy meal. More of your blood flow is being diverted to your stomach and intestines.

Finally all of the digested nutrients are absorbed through the intestinal walls. The waste products of this process include undigested parts of the food, known as fiber, and older cells that have been shed from the mucosa (intestinal lining). These materials are propelled into the colon, where they remain usually for a day or two until a bowel movement expels the feces.

Mrs. Samana

As we have seen, *Mrs. Samana* is the cook and lady of the house. In her kitchen, there is always a fire burning, as she runs around trying hard not to let the fire go out. She often puts her hands up in despair and says, "I'm as good as the ingredients I get. I can't make a silk purse out of a pig's ear!" Her voice is the rumbling in your stomach as she protests about poor quality food or the fact you just swallowed a whole glass of cold water on top of your food, diluting precious digestive acid. Without the right nutrients coming her way, she struggles to keep the fire ticking over. She tries her very best to create goodness out of the ingredients brought to her, but as she says, "No wood … no fire!" *Mrs. Samana* also requires peace and quiet when she is busy. If you are multitasking while eating or jump into action straight after a meal, *Mrs. Samana* will have difficulty focusing on her job. It is also no good giving her a heavy task late at night when she is supposed to be resting. She will find it difficult to muster up the energy needed to start the cooking and manifesting process. It is quite likely that she will only do half the job, leaving you with undigested food in your stomach for too long.

Mrs. Samana's messages are very clear when you are not giving her the resources to do this enormous job properly. You will quite likely suffer from indigestion, flatulence, heartburn, acid reflux, or constipation.

Mrs. Samana has the huge task of processing all of your food as well as your mind matter. She is the fire in your belly (the second brain), digesting and processing thoughts and emotions. It makes perfect sense to me that *Mrs. Samana* is behind your sixth sense, or your gut feelings.

Your sixth sense is organic. It lives and breathes within you, and when your body is tired and not working properly, *Mrs. Samana* cannot serve you. She then waits patiently for you to provide the right ingredients so she can assist with your mind-set and enable you to raise your awareness and be in tune with your gut feelings. When she is disabled, your lower mind takes over, and you may find yourself making poor quality choices, which will undoubtedly affect your sense of perception and reality.

Psychology of *Samana Vayu*

Now that you can see the role that good nutrition plays on your psychology, you will understand more about how, when you are tired, you may notice that you can't see the wood for the trees. You have no energy to make decisions or deal with confrontation. During times of stress, you may find that you lose your temper for no apparent reason. That will be the volcano of *samana* exploding. Unbalanced *samana* will loom over you like Mount Vesuvius does over the bay of Naples. One never quite knows when it will erupt next and bury you under the ash and lava of struggling *samana*. It can be quite unforgiving!

Low *samana* could also mean that you hide behind the stuff bubbling away under the surface and going against your gut instinct. You may be avoiding confrontation and not saying something that needs to be asserted in fear of upsetting someone. *Samana* burning brightly will burn away the old stuff that is not who you are. No more kidding yourself and trying to be a second-rate version of someone you are not. The fire of *samana* creates internal space so you can unveil your true self and shine splendidly. Imagine becoming you as you really are meant to be.

Samana is about balance and connection. Once you bring your life, body, and mind into equilibrium, you will find that you discover creativity and concentration that you never knew you were capable of. You may also find that you feel congruent and connected to your soul and sleep a lot better. The detoxifying energy of *apana vayu*, which we will discuss later, can only get rid of stuff that is prepared to be got rid of. Imagine trying to stuff more rubbish into a bin that is already full. If you are clinging to disempowering beliefs and toxic mental waste, there is no space for the new. *Samana* will help you process it all, learn the lessons, and move on. It will give you the positive aspects of perception, enabling you to discriminate and act accordingly instead of reacting irrationally. When you go to bed, there is no pillow as soft as a clear conscience and a relaxed mind.

Check your *samana* levels by asking yourself the following questions.

	Yes / No
Do I have a problem with collecting clutter?	
Do I avoid confrontation?	
Is my concentration limited?	
Do I find it difficult to make important decisions?	
Does food take ages to digest in my stomach?	
Do I say yes to please or avoid trouble?	
Do I find it difficult to find balance in my life?	
Does my stomach feel knotted up?	

How did you do? If you answered yes to one or more of these questions, you need to stoke the fire and get your strength up. Be selfish and good to yourself before it is too late. Ignite your spirit with a balance between movement and rest. Only you can do it!

Reflection and *Samana* Goals

Once you have answered the questions, take some time to reflect. Consider how you can use *Mrs. Samana* and her wisdom to help you set goals in connection with your digestive system. Remember that your ability to assimilate food and experience can impact the quality of your sleep.

Seeing	The purpose of *samana* is to digest anything that comes into your space, which includes experience so you see more clearly. Take notice of what you think you are seeing.
Appetite	Make sure you develop an appetite for healthy foods.
Mindful	Be mindful of where you spend your time. Try to make sure it is nourishing to your mind, heart, and soul.
Action	Take action and do all the exercises presented to you. No action means no result. Halfhearted action gives you a 50 per cent result, and 100 per cent action and effort will give you a great result!
No	Learn to say no when you need to. Say no to unhealthy food and situations that don't serve you.
Assimilate	Take time to assimilate things, and don't overload your mind or stomach. Take time out for lunch, and allow a little time for the digestion and assimilation of food before you run off to your next task. Allow your mind to rest by making meditation a daily ritual. Your mind will start to see things a lot more clearly given half the chance.

Now Set Your Goals

Write down your goals as if you have already achieved them. Here are some examples of how to get started:

- I took time to eat properly instead of eating on the go.
- I sat quietly for ten minutes after my main meal of the day.
- I dedicated this week to 100 per cent conscious eating.
- I ate lightly in the evening and before seven thirty every day this week.

Let's Get More *Samana*

Let me ask you a question: Do you feel fired up and ready to go or burned out and ready to drop? Invite *samana* to light your fire as follows. Read this all the way through once so you understand it. When you are ready, do the practice and write your reflections in your journal.

Discover the Fire of *Samana Vayu*

To find *samana vayu*, we can do this special *samana vayu* practice. The home of *samana* is at the navel, and the trigger point is three finger widths below the navel.

Find a seated comfortable position with your back straight. Become aware of the breath in the navel area. Just watch, feel, and notice any sensations. Now start focusing on the exhalation in particular, and consciously send the exhale down into the trigger point below the navel. You may notice that the area becomes very compact. When you are ready to inhale, inhale into the area above this point, and try to fill up the centre of the body only. This will require practice, but use the power of your intention to create the experience of energy drawing into your centre. This is your *samana vayu*. Practice this for ten breaths.

See: Visualisation and Simple Belly-Breathing Exercise

Let's start stoking the fire of *samana*. Set your timer for ten minutes. Lie on your back, and bring your awareness to your belly. As you inhale, imagine the fire of the sun streaming into your belly, and as you exhale, imagine all the waste dissolving into the earth. Allow the breathing to be natural. Don't try to control the breath. Just observe and visualise the solar energy being drawn into your solar plexus. Continue until the alarm goes off.

Feel: *Surya Bedhi,* Sun Breathing

We have already talked about the two halves of the human being: the left being related to the moon and the cooling qualities of the female and the right being related to the sun and the activity and heating qualities of the male. Sun breathing is a very powerful breathing exercise, especially if done in the morning. This exercise helps increase the internal fire, digest and release impurities, and revives your energy levels. Practice on an empty stomach.

Sit in a comfortable seated position with your spine straight. Raise your right hand, and create *Vishnu Mudra* by tucking in your first and middle fingers, leaving your pinky, ring finger, and thumb out. See page xxxxx for a reminder.

Close the left nostril with the ring finger of your right hand, and silently inhale through the right nostril. Hold the breath for a moment, close your right nostril with your thumb, and exhale through your left nostril. This is one round.

As you are inhaling, visualise the golden light of the sun. See the fire, and feel the warmth of the solar energy. Continue to inhale and completely fill yourself up with this breath. Repeat for five minutes.

Eat: *Samana* Food

Samana foods are nourishing and easy on the digestion, and they help a balanced digestion process, enabling your body to unlock the vitamins, minerals, calories, fats, and proteins you need. Some examples include live yogurt, whole grains, mung beans, oils such as ghee and sesame, ginger, and digestive spices like turmeric, cumin, coriander, and cloves.

Samana Affirmation

"I am igniting. I am purifying. I am luminous."

Reminder

- Remember: this is our first introduction to Mrs. Samana, and we are working our way through each of the vayus, getting to know each one in turn.
- Take your time, and try out all of the exercises as instructed.
- Write down your reflections and thoughts in your journal.
- This is the preparation for the five-week plan.
- You will find video resources for the exercises in this book at www.breathebettersleepbetter.co.uk
- You will find recipes for samana food at www.breathebetter sleepbetter.co.uk

Chapter 6

The Expansiveness of Vyana Vayu

"I was dead, then alive.
Weeping, then laughing.
The power of love came into me,
and I became fierce like a lion,
then tender like the evening star"

—Rumi

At times in my life, I have felt stuck, lacking in energy and without focus. It occurred to me that, as someone who was naturally claustrophobic, I needed lots of space to move. If I feel restricted physically or mentally, I don't feel good. I guess that is how *vyana* feels.

Many years ago, when I was a massage therapist doing treatments in a tiny room under the stairs in a gym, I did not feel good. Every time I moved round the massage table, I had to duck my head for fear of bashing it on the beams of the staircase. I was in that room for four years, dreaming of being in a big space. I remember chatting to one of my clients about life goals, and the word that came out was "freedom." Yes, I wanted to be free. Now that I have an understanding of *vyana*, I realise why stretching feels so good. We are making space for energy.

When you think about it, everything is connected energetically in one form or another. The universe is just energy and vibration. Energy needs to flow freely. Think of yourself as a battery. At one end you are negative; at the other end, you are positive. We work because we have an energy flow. Without it, we have inertia.

The energy of *vyana* flows both internally and externally, provided you give it enough space to move. It is connecting everything from your central core via a series of energy channels outwards. As we have seen in Eastern philosophy, these energy channels are called *nadis* or meridians, and they run through our entire system. Interestingly, in geography, a meridian is the same thing, a line that connects points around the Earth. Also consider the way in which the human circulatory system transports blood to every part of your body and back again. There is no end to the way that energy flows around the human system.

It's not hard to see that, when this system flows freely, we are full of vitality. And once it becomes weak or congested, we struggle with poor mental and physical health. The alchemy of *vyana* is that constant movement of universal energy inside of you. When it's working, it surrounds you, connects, and grounds you. That's when you feel balanced and integrated as a whole person instead of fragmented and disconnected.

Sadly, even with the best intentions, you may sometimes lose the connection to our energy source, which can be for all kinds of reasons. At some point though, like me, you will need to heed your inner voice, change your mind-set, and take control of your life, which you can do by giving yourself the space to breathe. You are a channel for universal energy, but if that energy is being drained, your personal effectiveness will be undermined.

When I am just surviving and not living fully, I have no energy. I am emotionally and spiritually detached from what I am doing. I feel as if I am withering on the vine. What does "just surviving" feel or look like to you? When you recognise it in yourself, look around. Can you sense who else's energy is depleted? What signs do you see or sense?

Remember that your light will get pulled towards the darkness when in the company of someone with low energy, a bit like positive and negative electrons always trying to move towards each other in an effort to create balance. The universal energy is constantly looking to find balance. It does not take responsibility for your supply. You have to do that yourself. The good news is that there are plenty of opportunities to find more *prana*. You just have to make the space for it.

When you have taken heed and listened to *prana* and *samana*, you will gain the strength and vitality required for sustained physical or mental activity. You will also find that you are more relaxed when you need to sleep. *Vyana* is omnipresent if allowed to be and will bring you the fuel to expand your horizons and think outside of the box. As you sit quietly and consider *vyana*, are you using and harnessing energy in this moment, or are you struggling to get through your day?

Something you may want to consider is stopping every once in a while during the day and just connecting to yourself and asking, "How is my energy right now?" Most of the time, we push on unconsciously without considering if we have the energy to continue. Our energy source becomes temporarily depleted, and we rely on adrenalin, the stress hormone, not *prana*. This is a bit like putting diesel in a petrol car. It won't take long before you have a breakdown.

Let me take you back to the height of my insomniac days, as I was stuck in a destructive marriage and unable to move and spread my wings. It was a bit like putting blocks on all my energetic channels. Energy did not flow, and I could not think or see further than the end of my nose. I was thinking small and playing small in those days, feeling like an insecure and inadequate mess. My *vyana* was certainly in a state of enormous stagnation.

In a Nutshell: *Vyana Vayu*, the Heart of the Matter

Vyana means expansion, and it is the energy that allows you to be open. Imagine *vyana* as the midday sun and the height of summer. It's the activity of growth and moves outwards towards the light. If there are blocks among the energy rivers and streams of the body, it can't expand, but when it flows freely, your mind and heart will open like a flower with a thousand petals. *Vyana*, therefore, relates to the element of air and sense of touch. You can touch only a few people with your hands, but thousands with the energy and wisdom of your heart. *Vyana* longs for freedom and, given the energy it requires, it goes beyond boundaries, energising and cleansing anything in its path.

Vyana asks you to connect and listen to your inner wisdom, which gives you intuition and insight. It is the part of you that truly knows you, but which may continue to elude you. When you are ungrounded, your connection to your energy sources will waver. Remember the idea of tuning into that *pranic* radio station. You need to fiddle to find a clear and strong signal before you can start drawing on the energy of *prana*. You might find it hard to get that feeling straight away, as feeling is often difficult for those of us who live in our heads and not our hearts, running constantly towards this goal or that. I used to struggle with this, but with time and practice, it does get easier to travel inwards and see, sense, feel, and just know what is going on.

The Role of *Vyana*

Vyana is the energetic transport department, and it all starts with the heart. I suspect, if I told you that heart disease is the number-one killer and claims approximately one million lives per year[3] in the United States, you may be surprised. Let's add a bit more perspective to that. Approximately every three seconds, someone dies of a cardiovascular-related disease, which is like the September 11 tragedy repeating itself every 24 hours, 365 days per year. Worldwide we are looking at 17 million people per year. That is an awful lot of people with circulatory issues.

I find it inconceivable that we have so little respect for our heart. Even the ancient Egyptians understood that the heart is something more than a physical organ. They believed the heart was the centre of everything. During the mummification process, they actually pulled out the brain through the nose and chucked it away, but they took great care to leave the heart in the body, as they felt that the heart contained the essence of everything the person is or was.

To give you an example of how powerful the heart is and how connected it is to *prana*, if you took it out of the body but continued to give it oxygen, it would actually continue to beat. It's an interesting thought if you think of the electrical and magnetic field we were talking about when discussing *prana* in chapter xxx.

Vyana's role is comparable to the cardiovascular and lymphatic circulatory system. It is always on the move, trying to make its way through pathways to get stuff to where it needs to be. Imagine the body's circulatory system made up of arteries, capillaries, and veins laid out in one long piece. It comes to about sixty thousand miles or one hundred thousand kilometres. The circumference of the earth is twenty-five thousand miles or forty thousand kilometres, which means we could wrap ourselves around the world more than twice with our circulatory system. What we are talking about here is the seventy-two thousand *nadis* (energetic channels) through which our *pranic* energy flows. If our physical being is that large, think how large our energetic field must be.

The quality of *vyana's* work is very much reliant on what *prana* brings in and how well *samana* prepares nutrients for sending out. *Vyana* is not going to be able to carry heavy, negative weight in the same way as light positivity around the *nadi* system. Imagine going for a hike with a ten-kilometre rucksack and then with a half-kilo bum bag. You would find the trip much easier with the latter and less likely to give up.

Vyana also depends on the free-flowing energy channels of the cardiovascular circulatory system. Clogged-up arteries and veins are like water trickling down a stream with stones blocking the way. The stones start going green as pockets of water get trapped. Soon enough the water becomes dirty and starts to smell. Atherosclerosis is comparable to a blocked-up energy system. The collection of cholesterol and other matter starts narrowing the pathway, making the arteries harder, less flexible, and liable to malfunction altogether.

The free-flowing energy of *vyana* makes sure that oxygen-enriched blood travels to your heart, ready to be pumped around the body so the red blood cells can reach their destinations. *Vyana's* energy is also responsible for delivering nutrients from your food as well as hormones from the glands. It also drives the metabolic waste collection to ensure that toxic waste does not remain in the body. Provided it flows freely, your body will be well nourished, energised, and kept in working order. If the current of *vyana* is lethargic and lacks its exclusive characteristic of fluidity, you will feel flat, small, and rather fed up. Your inner being will be rattling your cage most likely when you are trying to sleep. Use this sleeplessness as a sign that something needs to change. There is always a message in the inability to sleep.

Mr Vyana

Mr Vyana is a great friend to have. He will always be at the centre (heart) of things, keeping the channels of communication with the other *vayus* open. When his path is blocked, you become blocked, and *Mr Vyana* will struggle to pick you up and guide you on your way. As a result, your get-up-and-go will get up and go, and you will get that heavy heart feeling. Also when you feel lethargic, it's hard to know which way to turn. If your heart can't expand, neither can you. *Mr Vyana* has a huge heart and is extremely generous and loving. And he is a beautiful, compassionate spirit. He absolutely hates it when people try to put him in a box and constrain him. He is a free thinker and likes to get out and about. *Mr Vyana* is all about expansion and change. Anywhere you go, you will always bump into *Mr Vyana* wearing his comfortable and unrestricted clothing and carrying his intuitive heart compass. He is always on the move and, by nature, always moving and growing. Everyone loves *Mr Vyana*.

Mr Vyana relies on you to purify your body and mind so he does not come face-to-face with blocked channels, which may prevent him from getting to the farthest corners of the body.

Psychology of *Vyana Vayu*

Vyana is the world's best antidepressant. Increasing *vyana* will bring you a sense of joy and openness, the kind of sensation you may feel walking in the breeze on a vast, sandy beach, looking outwards to an infinite, deep blue ocean. It will make you feel alive and full of love. It is associated with giving and sharing and begins at the heart as it shines out like a sunbeam to the rest of the world. Imagine those seventy-two thousand *nadis* radiating outwards full of *prana*.

Vyana promotes mental circulation, creativity, and free-flowing ideas. It will allow you to think big and reach out to the secret corners of your imagination. You need *vyana* to expand and open the mind. It will give agility, freedom, and fresh energy to inspire you. You may admire people who always seem to be moving forwards, doing new things in their lives. These people have removed the boundaries, restricting them by allowing *vyana* to move. *Vyana* produces the possibility of growth, creativity, and spirituality and gives you the feeling of being connected to the rest of the world. It stimulates your desire for personal freedom and opens your heart.

If you are feeling low or anxious, it means you have disconnected yourself from the universal spirit and become separate and small. You need to break the external barriers you have put around yourself by doing things that expand the mind, body, and breath.

Check your *vyana* levels by asking yourself the following questions.

	Yes/ No
Do I feel big and expansive?	
Do I consider myself a generous person?	
Do I feel connected and alive?	
Am I able to let my hair down and enjoy myself?	
Am I able to think outside the box?	
Do I consider myself an open-hearted person?	
Do I forgive easily?	

How did you do? If you answered no to one or more of these questions, I have one word for you, space. Go outside and get going. Walk, run, or go by car, if you can't walk. Look to the horizon. Take in what you see. Dissolve your limitations. Replace "cannots" with "cans."

Do something you have never done before. Expand the mind, body, and spirit. Loosen that hard external skin and break through.

Reflection and *Vyana* Goals

Once you have answered the questions, take some time to reflect. Consider how you can use *Mr Vyana* and his wisdom to help you set goals to continue your journey of personal growth and a great night's sleep.

Value	Value yourself and your own feelings.
Yes	Say yes to life and break free from being small.
Affirmations	Affirmations are so powerful. You have to do them for anything to happen. Make affirmations part of your daily practice.
Nature	Get out in nature. Sit on a mountaintop, look out to sea, or take a room with a view. Get out into open spaces, breathe the fresh air, and notice how refreshed and free you feel.
Amore	Most people know the word *amore*, which means "love" in Italian. Work at bringing your awareness into your heart at various points during the day. As soon as you make that connection, your breath will deepen, and you will feel more connected to compassion and love.

Now Set Your Goals

Write down your goals as if you have already achieved them. Here are some examples to get you started:

- I got out in nature three times a week.
- I stepped outside of my comfort zone and booked myself in for a new experience.

- I reached out to someone I have been thinking about for a long time.

Let's Get More *Vyana*

Let me ask you a question: Do you feel stuck and unable to move? Invite *vyana* to help you make space. Read this all the way through once so you understand it. When you are ready, do the practice and write your reflections in your journal.

Discover the Expansiveness of *Vyana Vayu*

Let's find *vyana vayu* in your body. *Vyana vayu* resides in the heart centre. Everything flows to and from the heart, and *vyana vayu* reaches out to the very edges of our personal aura and more.

Find your comfortable seated position with your back straight, and inhale as if your whole body was one enormous lung. Exhale through every single pore of your body, and imagine you are exhaling towards the centre of the body. At the very end of the exhale, when you are empty, subtly hold the breath for a moment, and inhale with the same sensation through every pore of the skin. Your body will feel like you are becoming lighter and less dense. It is a wonderful floating feeling. Practice this for ten breaths.

See: Visualisation Exercise

Find your comfortable seated position and start by just closing your eyes and following your breath for a few moments. When you feel that you are centred and quiet, start imagining that you are inhaling divine light, energy, and love in through the crown of your head, deep into the centre of your heart. When your lungs are full, hold the breath for a couple seconds. Then exhale through the back of your lungs and imagine you are sending love to anything and everything behind you. Continue for ten breaths.

Now, still inhaling divine light, energy, and love through the crown of your head, when your lungs are full, hold the breath for a few seconds, and exhale out the left side of your lungs, sending love to anything and everything to the left of you. Continue for ten breaths. Continue to inhale through the crown of your head, hold for a couple seconds, and exhale love to anything and everything to the right of you. Repeat for ten breaths.

Now inhale through the crown of your head, hold for a couple seconds, and exhale out of the front of your heart, sending love to anything and everything in front of you. Repeat for ten breaths. Finally continue to inhale divine light, energy, and love through the crown of your head. Hold for a couple seconds, and exhale equally out the front, back, and sides of your heart, sending love out to everyone and everything. Continue for five minutes. You may experience a feeling of strength in your heart or a feeling of a connection to the spirit. Enjoy this. It's marvelous!

Feel: The Breath of Joy

The following exercise will have you feeling good in a jiffy. It wakes up the circulatory system and opens the chest. Stand up with your feet hip-width apart. Inhale quickly and sharply, and at the same time, swing your arms up in front of you. Now swing your arms out to the side of you with another sharp, quick inhale. The exhale from the previous inhale will have looked after itself. Don't think about it. Just think about the inhale.

Now swing your arms up in front of you again with a quick, sharp inhale. Hold the breath for a couple seconds, and exhale strongly and fully as you swing your arms down. Bend your knees at the same time. You can bend your knees as deeply as comfortable. If you have problems with your back, just do the arms, and work up to adding in the legs. The more effort you put in, the better you will feel. Do it fully and with all your heart and smile. Try it for ten breaths.

Eat: *Vyana* Foods

Vyana foods hydrate and add water. In addition to drinking plenty of water, the following are some examples: cucumber, iceberg lettuce, celery, tomatoes, cauliflower, strawberries, watermelon, and spinach.

Vyana Affirmation

"I am expansive and in the flow of life."

> *Reminder*
>
> - *Remember that this is our first introduction to Mr Vyana, and we are working our way through each of the vayus, getting to know each one in turn.*
> - *Take your time and try out all of the exercises as instructed.*
> - *Write down your reflections and thoughts in your journal.*
> - *This is the preparation for the five-week plan.*
> - *You will find video resources for the exercises in this book at www.breathebettersleepbetter.co.uk*
> - *You will find recipes for vyana food at www.breathebetter sleepbetter.co.uk*

Chapter 7

The Cleansing Power of *Apana Vayu*

"Last night I lost the world, and gained the universe"

—C JoyBell C

At the end of summer when autumn approaches, I feel a sense of wanting to declutter, get rid of cobwebs and dust, let in fresh air, and release the hot, sticky summer (although I guess that depends on which country you live in). Even though I adore the summer sun because it makes everyone feel so positive, something about autumn makes everything smell and taste differently. Maybe it's the earthy colors that bring me back down to earth after the whirlwind of the sociable summer sun. It's certainly a time when I want to connect to nature, get out in the woods, or tend the garden.

As autumn progresses, the colors change, and the leaves drop. My walks in the countryside invariably induce a feeling of release. Not a crash, bang, or wallop letting go. It's more of a letting things naturally find their own way. A tapestry of rich mahogany, chestnut, and earthy brown shades adorn the ground, creating a carpet of exquisite beauty. When the leaves crunch underfoot and the air becomes sharper, reaching deep into my lungs, I feel so alive.

At these times I am at my most reflective, as if my mind is asking me to move the rubbish that occupies my thoughts through my body and let them seep into Mother Earth. From there she can transport them away to the place where they can be transformed and recycled into something more positive and useful.

Sometimes when I am in nature, I stand and imagine that I am a tree that is part of the forest. When my roots are in place, I listen very carefully. Oddly, at these times, it is as if there is no other life, just me and silence. As I imagine my breath leaving my body through my roots, I know I am expelling everything that I no longer need. In those moments I am grounded, have a sense of purpose, and feel I can trust and let go instead of hanging on to habits that don't serve me.

It took me a long time to move on from my first divorce. I was very young then. What I came to realise was that, until I let it go, there would be no space for the new, and I would continue to move in an ever-decreasing vicious circle. When you are hanging on to stuff, your digestive fire will struggle to burn with any efficiency, which in turn sends a flurry of misinformation to the mind and clouds your judgment.

In 2005, I was at a point where I knew something had to change, and I jetted myself off to a physical and spiritual cleansing retreat and seminar in Fiji. The place itself, Namale, was paradise, and I will surely go back there one day. This seminar could not have come at a better time, as I was truly ready for the mental, physical, and spiritual purification that it was offering.

Every day of the seminar, we were recommended to have a colonic irrigation, which, for the uninitiated, means washing out your colon with warm water. Because of what we eat, our colons invariably get all kinds of fecal matter stuck to the sides and in all of the crevices. When matter gets stuck, we can't digest things properly, and toxins seep into our bodies, causing all kinds of damage.

For the first two colonic irrigation treatments, I was letting go of very little, which I found hugely frustrating, but when day three came after a bit of persuasion from all that clean water, things really started to move. I had no idea there was so much stuff hanging about inside of me. It promoted a huge emotional breakthrough, and I felt totally liberated. I was incredibly fragile that day, and I broke down in tears constantly for what I perceived as no reason at all. This is a great example of the interconnection between the physical, mental, and spiritual level. A blockage on any of these planes results in obstacles everywhere.

At Namale, there was also a stunning spa on a volcanic cliff on the edge of a rain forest where you could just look out to a pure aquamarine sea from the spa windows. In addition to the colonic treatments, we were advised to have massage, which helps the body's natural detoxification process. We were also juice fasting for the five days, only drinking vegetable juices, a couple servings of a couple of lettuce leaves, and avocado and water. The whole process was magical, and perhaps that will be a subject for another book, but suffice to say, there was a huge shedding on all levels of my being.

As each day passed, I felt the layers falling away, bit by bit, until all that was left was the real, authentic me. I felt completely present, full of love and warmth, and in particular, there was no internal negative chatter. I felt as though I was plugged into some sort of gigantic cosmic electricity supply. On the last evening, as the sun set, I knew I was allowing the sun to set on my past, and by morning, when the sun rose again, things would be very different. And they definitely were.

Let's look for a moment at the process of letting go. As you know from the *samana* chapter, everything that comes into our space from the five senses. Anything that passes our lips, including the air we breathe, goes through a digestive process.

First *samana* breaks it all down into good, keep, and throw away. Anything that will hold you back or interfere with the ability to produce creative energy for your activities in the world will go into the "throw away pile." There may be some resistance to the letting go of things that you once perceived to give you pleasure, when actually they were creating disease in your system. This may be a destructive relationship, for example, smoking, drinking, eating junk food, or something subtler. There comes a time when the penny drops, and you decide that it's time.

Following that resolution, there is the actual process of release. First there's the breaking down or dissecting of the thing holding you back. Next there's a paradoxical kind of yearning to hang on to it because you feel safer in your small box. You then take the leap of faith and experiment with the experience of not hanging on to anything. The surrender happens next as you navigate your newfound freedom. A wonderful feeling of lightness follows. You might even lose a few pounds in the process.

In the practice of yoga, one of the most frequently studied principles is the concept of letting go. There is a special word for it, *vairagaya*, which means "dispassion," "surrender," and "letting go." When you hold on to something so tightly, terrified of its loss, energy will no longer flow, and it will result in self-destruction. Once you focus on being more peaceful and surrendering to wherever you are right now rather than where you would rather be, something wonderful happens. *Prana* actually starts to flow.

In a Nutshell: *Apana Vayu, Prana Vayu's* Other Half

Apana is the sunset, as *prana* is the sunrise. The inhale (*prana*) and exhale (*apana*) work together just like the sunrise and sunset. *Apana* is the autumn and the energy that turns the leaves of the trees brown. It enables them to drop to the earth gradually, dissolving them into the ground. It is the energy of elimination and detoxification that allows us the space to bring in the new. *Apana* governs the directional force of gravity. It keeps us rooted to the earth. Imagine how a tree grows up towards the light. For as much as it grows upwards, it also grows downwards. *Apana* is the stability of a mighty oak tree.

Apana and *prana* move together like a couple doing the tango. The two halves move in complete harmony. While one supports the other, the forward move is stabilised by the backward move and vice versa. The two dancers are deeply connected and in love. Create the dance in your mind. The male dancer, beautifully fit with a lean body, leads the female, delicate, precise, and goddess-like. Whatever direction they move in, the pair never loose contact. *Prana* and *apana* are a beautiful dance of nature.

The Role of *Apana*

Apana is the out-breath, the cleansing and releasing breath that allows you to eliminate the carbon dioxide created from the gaseous exchange and digestion process done by *samana*. One thinks breathing is just about getting oxygen into the system, but breathing is also about expelling carbon dioxide and water. You don't just lose water when you sweat and pee. You lose water with each of the 21,600 breaths you breathe each day.

Apana is in charge of cleansing. The world is in trouble because of its careless disposal of waste, and so will you be. As an example of careless waste disposal, in Campania, southern Italy, serious and illegal dumping of toxic waste has caused a significant rise in liver cancer. The national average is 14 per 100,000, but in Campania, it went up to 34.5 for men and 20.8 for women.[5]

Of course, someone was trying to keep it quiet, but as the earth never lies, neither does the body. This area in Italy now is referred to as the triangle of death. They tried to create quick fix fires to get rid of this waste, but as you and I both know, quick fixes don't really work. In fact, they just spread the poisons out into the environment even more.

Poorly digested food will start shouting sooner or later. Don't be fooled by those antacids either. You need acid in the stomach to digest food properly. Putting out the digestive fire won't help; finding the root cause and taking the appropriate steps will. You may find that your digestive problems will disappear with a few extra digestive herbs, an improved diet, and a positive mind-set.

It could be argued that the health of the digestive system is the single-most important long-term aspect of your health and well-being. *Ayurveda* (a form of Indian medicine meaning the science of life) tells us that a healthy digestive system leads to a healthy life and an unhealthy digestive system leads to disease. Even Western doctors would agree with that. When your digestion is compromised, so is your immune system and overall health. *Apana* is the foundation of your immune system, and weak *apana* contributes to most chronic illness. That makes lots of sense to me.

The immune system is designed to defend you against millions of bacteria, viruses, toxins, and parasites that would love to invade your body and turn it upside down. It never stops working in the background, but when it does get compromised, we certainly know about it. Colds and infections will constantly attack us until our energy is robbed and we have to slow down and take stock.

Apana governs the lower part of the body and is also particularly important for childbirth and menstruation. The cycle of pregnancy and childbirth is another incredible example of birth, growth, and release. Until menopause, each month, women's bodies typically go through a twenty-eight- to thirty-day period of preparing the womb for a child, which, if an egg is not fertilised, results in a bleed, a letting go of the womb's lining. When an egg is fertilised, the letting go is the act of bringing new life into the world and, of course, a new phase in your life as you move into motherhood.

Mr Apana

Mr Apana, as we have seen, is the waste disposal department, and it is his job to expel impurities and toxic waste while conserving the nourishing stuff. If I had to describe him, he is strong and stocky in build with a big heart and incredible integrity. He is our protector and tirelessly removes all our waste and toxins. His modest presence sniffs out the bad and kicks it out without a second thought. He is a no-nonsense kind of character and will not tolerate filth. *Mr Apana* is extremely active and uses up an awful lot of energy doing his job with enthusiasm and vigor. If *Mr Prana* is unable to bring in the life force, none of his team can function, including *Mr Apana*.

He also needs time to cleanse his equipment properly and relies on the right cleaning materials to do that job. For example, a regular supply of apple cider vinegar would be extremely useful for its cleansing properties. Foods like avocado for its soluble fiber content, flax and chia seeds for their fiber and fatty acids, and green fruits and vegetables rich in healthy digestion-promoting chlorophyll will all be gratefully received first by *Mrs Samana*, followed by *Mr Apana*.

Psychology of *Apana Vayu*

Blockages in any area of the body will fog up the mind. *Apana* is the energy that allows you to declutter your mind. When working at full capacity, *apana* eliminates the negative by-products of emotional and mental experience, which, if not digested properly, become a source of toxicity. When in balance, *apana* enables you to detach and maintain equanimity in the face of trauma and upset. Imagine *apana* as your mental digestive system and the energy that keeps you rooted and grounded.

When *apana* is out of sorts and weak, you will feel heavy, stifled, and languid. You may find yourself feeling insecure and fearful, especially in your relationships with others. If you think of that tree, when the wind blows, the branches and leaves move freely without uprooting it. When life gets hairy, you remain flexible and move with the wind as *apana* keeps you deeply embedded in the earth and the mind free from attachment.

Living in clutter and storing things for a rainy day that will never come is a sign of low *apana* energy. It's time to detox the house and get rid of stuff that isn't beautiful or useful. You will feel liberated and so much lighter.

Check your *apana* levels by asking yourself the following questions.

	Yes/ No
I have a tendency to bear grudges.	
I hoard lots of things and live in clutter.	
I have a tendency not to finish things before I start new ones.	
I find it difficult to let go of anything.	
I have difficulty in going to the bathroom daily and have irregular bowel movements.	
I am regularly constipated.	
I suffer from a lot of gas.	

How did you do? Make a note in your journal of the things you need to work on, and make sure you take action. For example, spring-clean, detox your system, declutter your day, and remove unnecessary, unproductive tasks from your to-do list. And get a problem off your chest by talking to a friend or writing about it, allowing the stream of consciousness to just flow onto a piece of paper. I invite you to work on your *apana* energy by doing the following.

Reflection and *Apana* Goals

Once you have answered the questions, take some time to reflect. Consider how you can use *Mr Apana* and his wisdom to set goals that directly connect with your ability to let go that which does not serve you. *Apana* is the sunset. At bedtime, for anything that is going around and around in your mind, abandon to your journal. As you drift off to sleep, your unconscious mind can assimilate the day and revive you for the next.

Abandon	Abandon activities, relationships, and eating habits that don't serve you!
Prayer	Saying a short prayer of gratitude before we eat helps us appreciate our food, eat with more attention, and assimilate the food better.
Attention	Pay attention to how well food is going through your system.
Nighttime	Eating late in the evening will affect the quality of your sleep.
Apple cider vinegar	This is an amazing digestive aid and an old-fashioned remedy that works. Ditch the digestive aids, and try a dessert spoon of apple cider vinegar in a drop of warm water before you eat.

Now Set Your Goals

Write down your goals as if you have already achieved them. Here are some examples to get you started:

- I decluttered the whole house and feel amazing for it.
- I changed my perspective on X and let it all go.

Let's Get More *Apana*

Let me ask you a question. Do you feel mentally blocked and physically listless? Invite *apana* to help you let go. Read this all the way through once so you understand it. When you are ready, do the practice and write your reflections in your journal.

Discover and Open the Door of *Apana Vayu*

To find *apana vayu*, we can do this special *apana vayu* practice. The home of *apana* is the area below the navel, and the trigger point is the anus.

Find a seated comfortable position with your back straight. Become aware of the sensations in the area of the anus. Now start focusing on the exhale. As you exhale, contract the anus slowly until you have exhaled completely and your lungs are empty. Hold the breath out for a few moments. Then imagine you are inhaling into the lower belly as you release and relax the anus downwards. You may notice that there is an expansion downwards towards the pelvic floor and maybe a bit above it. This is your *apana vayu* working. Practice this for ten breaths.

See: Visualisation Exercise

Find a comfortable seated position on a chair or the floor. The important thing is to be comfortable. Let the mind rest where the body touches the earth, and intensify the sensations of the body sinking into the earth. Notice the sensation of downward movement flowing through the body. Think of your body as a tree. The more the branches and leaves reach up and out towards the light, the more your roots equally reach down deep into the earth. Visualise yourself letting negative mental weight and toxins dissolve downward while you start to feel lighter and freer. Intensify further the grounding and rooting sensation while at the same time the spine lengthens with new lightness and space. Do this exercise for ten minutes.

Feel: *Kapalabhati Kriya*

Kapalabhati Kriya or "shining skull breath" is a cleansing breath that cleanses the breathing apparatus, tones the digestive system, purifies the blood, and refreshes the brain. It is an excellent practice for letting go of the old. To perform *Kapalabhati Kriya*, you need to be seated with your back straight. Keep your mouth closed. We are doing this exercise using the nose only. Once you are in a comfortable position, close your eyes and inhale. And as you exhale, imagine you are blowing out a candle with your nose. Now repeat quickly, not thinking about the inhale at all as that will look after itself. Just keep exhaling with the forced exhale. Continue for twenty seconds. At the end of the round, keep your eyes closed and take a few long deep breaths. Do this for three rounds.

This exercise is contraindicated if you are pregnant or have high blood pressure, heavy periods, a heavy cold, headache, an ear infection, or an IUD contraceptive device.

Eat: *Apana* Foods

Apana foods and herbs help food move through the intestines and, in particular, foods that are high in fiber. Oils are also helpful in the cleansing process as it helps prevent constipation. They include the earthy winter-type foods, for example, carrots and root vegetables; beans; dried fruits like dates, figs, prunes, apricots, and raisins; whole grains; broccoli; fruits like plums, pears, and apples; soaked almonds (easier to digest if soaked); oils like ghee and sesame; omega-3 oils like oily fish or seed options like Udos oil (available online); or Triphala, an Ayurvedic herb coming from three fruits: Harada, Amla, and Bihara (available on most Ayurvedic online).

Apana **Affirmation**

"I let go. I let go. I let go."

> Reminder
>
> - Remember that this is our first introduction to Mr Apana and we are working our way through each of the vayus, getting to know each one in turn.
> - Take your time and try out all of the exercises as instructed.
> - Write down your reflections and thoughts in your journal.
> - This is the preparation for the five-week plan.
> - You will find video resources for the exercises in this book at www.breathebettersleepbetter.co.uk
> - You will find recipes for apana food at www.breathebetter sleepbetter.co.uk

Chapter 8

Majestic *Udana*

"Strength does not come from physical capacity. It comes from an indomitable will"

—Mahatma Gandhi

Life is not always neat and tidy. Things go up, down, sideways and, sometimes even with the best will in the world, completely upside down. I remember a difficult time when I was very stressed and suffering with insomnia. I just could not get anything done. My body felt stiff, my hair was falling out, and I had lost the ability to think clearly. Negative thoughts were going over and over in my head, and as you can imagine, I was not feeling well. Everything I turned my hand to seemed to fail. I felt I had lost any hope of being creative and successful. To make matters worse, when I tried to explain how I was feeling, I couldn't get anything out. It just festered inside of me.

I believe this was the cause of my thyroid issue. Let's look for a moment at the function of the thyroid. The thyroid is in charge of metabolism, converting nutrients into energy. It also regulates body temperature, helps digestion, and contributes to our cognitive ability. The thyroid gland secretes three vital hormones: thyroxine (T4), triiodthyronine (T3), and calcitonin. The T3 and T4 work to balance metabolism, and calcitonin regulates calcium in the body, which obviously affects our bone-building process.

We need iodine for this concoction of hormones to do their job, which many of us are lacking due to the depletion of our soil. The work of the thyroid impacts all the creative work in our body, for example, protein, building muscle, and producing energy. *Udana* is the subtle nectar of the thyroid gland, and if depleted or nonexistent, thyroid problems are very likely. It is no surprise, therefore, that I managed to push myself so close to my limit that I developed the autoimmune disease, Hashimoto's thyroiditis.

I wish I knew then what I know now. I might have listened more to that inner nagging voice begging me to express myself and get it out. If you have had conversations with other people, especially women, with thyroid problems, you may find that they too have had confrontational issues. It is likely they are unable to express themselves for fear of upsetting someone else and strangling themselves like I did. I remember I would avoid conflict at all costs, as I knew I would be easily overpowered by others and just give up. I had no reserve strength, and this inability to speak was extremely debilitating. I realised I had lost my will to express myself. Like the cowardly lion in *The Wizard of Oz*, the words would not come. When I felt wronged, I dared not say what was really on my mind, in case I offended someone. Eventually I noticed that I became incapable of providing feedback because I was fearful of what others might think. My life became like a dull winter's day—bare, bleak, and frozen in an endless cycle of not sleeping and not functioning. This is *udana* completely out of whack.

Some of you may have seen the movie *The King's Speech* about the downtrodden prince with a terrible speech impediment who became King George VI of England. It was not until he overcame his fear by letting all that suppressed energy out that he was able to find his voice.

A timid, frightened king became a great leader for a country facing war. I recommend anyone to see the movie if you need inspiration. When *udana* is functioning at its highest, that's when you are able to voice your needs from a place of truth.

The voice is a like a musical instrument. When you sing, things happen. The feel-good endorphins start coming out to play, together with the stress-relieving oxytocin, whose levels, as an aside, are also driven up by hugging and kissing.

Singing improves your posture, which is interesting, as the directional force of *udana* is up towards the light, so one could say that singing increases confidence and mental awareness. When you feel good, you are much more alert. As singing reduces stress, you will also find that you sleep better after a good old singsong, even if you do your own karaoke show. A friend told me, for a short period, she was having singing lessons so she could learn to express herself and find her power again. She described that it felt as if she were reconnecting to a part inside of her that she had lost, the fragment that asks you to listen to your intuition and to speak your truth. This reminded me that voice is so much more than the sounds you make. If you have the strength to let it, it is the core of authentic creativity.

In a Nutshell: *Udana Vayu,* the Creator

Udana, the centre of cosmic sound, speech, and vibration, is responsible for vitality and strength. It is the result of the work done by *prana, samana, apana,* and *vyana.* Udana is the growth of consciousness and is translated as 'air that flies upwards'. Think lightness and levitation, and you have *udana.* It is the quiet space of midnight and the death of winter when things are asleep, renewing and preparing to move towards the light. Its subtle energy is deeply connected to the soul, leading it to the astral planes after death. *Udana* is ether and the vibration of sound, and when in balance, your soul and spirit will sing and dance with the excitement of the new season. It transforms the elements as they ascend from earth to water, to fire, to air, and then to space as *apana* would govern the downward transformation of the elements from space, to air, to fire, to water, and then to earth.

The Role of *Udana*

Udana imbues you with courage and the ability to confront your fears with confidence. Courage comes in many sizes and shapes, from confronting the hairy spider to making a sacrifice for your business or family or finding the courage to ask for help. Fear is an unpleasant emotion or thought. It is the feeling you get when you are afraid or worried that something bad is going to happen. Fear can be real or imaginary, and you often unnecessarily experience it because of your misperception or misjudgment of a situation. It causes you to feel anxiety, insecurity, and a complete lack of positive feelings. When we sense danger, real or imaginary, our body reacts, and fear can irrationally creep up on us. If you are well and functioning properly, *udana* will be ready to help you stand your ground with pride and integrity.

Udana is the energy that keeps you upright. In fact it keeps you standing. It gives you marvelous posture and a sense of lightness as it holds your head steady. *Udana* is the energy that keeps you moving and governs movement from the navel to the head. Once your body has taken energy in, digested it, sent it round, and got rid of the waste, it is now ready for action. Your *udana* energy is only as good as the work of the other four *vayus*. It is using the fuel created by the synchronicity of *prana, samana, vyana,* and *apana. Udana* is the energy that gets you up in the morning and inspires you to do things. Low *udana* means you won't feel like doing much. High *udana* will make you feel like you have something behind you, propelling you forward in the world.

Udana governs the growth of the body and cell renewal. Whatever you are producing in the world could be equated to beans on toast coming out of the kitchen or a wonderful feast of fresh and colorful vegetables prepared and cooked into the most beautiful meal. That is the difference between healthy *udana* and unhealthy *udana*. Another telltale sign is the quality of your sleep. If you are sleeping badly, *udana* is flagging and is unable to transport you to deep sleep and dream states. Once you are satisfied with what you have achieved during the day and feel fulfilled, you will sleep like a baby. When all *pranas* are balanced, everything works as it should.

Lord Udana

You will know the mighty *Lord Udana* as soon as you come into contact with him. That is why I decided to elevate him to Lord rather than Mr He is the epitome of truth, light, and courage. His posture is superb, fresh-faced, and joyous. There is an air about *Lord Udana*. He holds his head up high and is never afraid to stand up for what he believes in. Perhaps that is where the expression "hold your head up high" comes from. *Lord Udana* seems fearless and always has the courage to act from a standpoint of deep integrity. He does what he has to do and what is right.

Lord Udana takes full responsibility for our personal development and is a huge inspiration to everyone. He has a unique voice that is clear and concise whenever he is communicating. It's guaranteed that whatever he says comes from his heart. Everyone loves and trusts *Lord Udana* and looks to him for leadership and inspiration.

Psychology of *Udana Vayu*

Udana is in charge of what is possible. It is our evolving force and moves us to a higher sphere, encouraging us to rise up and grow. *Udana* keeps our spirits up and gives us the ability to be creative. It is the vital energy in the throat and invites you to express your higher self authentically. The energy of *udana* is behind who you are becoming and gives you mental energy and strength. Although *udana* is your voice, it will also give you permission not to speak until you are ready, so when you do express yourself, you do so with power and congruency. We all have a unique sound that comes from our vocal cords. As we exhale, we are able to speak, sing, or just make noise.

When *udana* becomes out of balance, you may find that you are unable to articulate your feelings and use words meaningfully. It is when you hear yourself say that you are too exhausted to talk. When someone says "I was just speechless," he or she probably felt that he or she did not have the energy to express how he or she felt in the face of a shocking situation. It requires energy to express and articulate what is coming from the depths of the heart, and it is sometimes not easy. Often when you feel powerless, you become speechless.

Check your *udana* levels by asking yourself the following questions.

	Yes/No
I tend to say yes to please for fear of upsetting people.	
I find it difficult to be congruent, and my words don't reflect my thoughts.	
I tend to sleep lightly and find I don't go into a deep, nourishing sleep.	
I often feel that I shrink down rather than rise to the challenge.	
I am more of a follower than a leader.	
I don't feel very creative.	
I find it hard to get inspired.	

How did you do? Make a note in your journal of the things you need to work on, and make sure you take action. For example, get inspired by writing down an uncensored goal list. (Think big!) Work on your posture through yoga, and sing more often!

Reflection and *Udana* Goals

Once you have answered the questions, take some time to reflect. Consider how you can use *Lord Udana* and his wisdom to help you set goals that connect you to your inner voice and continue your journey to personal growth and a good night's sleep.

Upwards	Stand tall and proud. Feel like you are making more space between each of the vertebrae in your spine. Improving your posture will enhance your confidence to be who you really are.
Daily	Not only will stretching your body daily make space in your body, it will create space in your mind for creativity.
Appreciate	Appreciate your blessings, and say it out loud. Tell someone you love how much you appreciate him or her. People sometimes need to hear it.
Noise	Get out of the noise and make solitude a regular part of your week. It will give you the space to think clearly and listen to your inner voice.
Authentic	Be authentic with your words and actions. Cultivating *udana* energy will help you communicate your truth.

Now Set Your Goals

Write down your goals as if you have already achieved them. Here are some examples to get you started:

- I said what was in my heart this week.
- I did yoga every morning.
- I started my most pressing creative project this week.

Let's Get More *Udana*

Let me ask you a question. How creative and energetic do you feel? Invite the wisdom of *udana* to get your creative juices flowing. Read this all the way through once so you understand it. When you are ready, do the practice, and write your reflections in your journal.

Discover the Victorious *Udana Vayu*

Udana's home and trigger point is the throat. Let's find our comfortable seated position with the spine straight and get ready to work with *udana vayu*. First just observe the breath. In particular, observe the breath in the area of the throat. Now take a long, deep inhale and focus on the throat as you exhale. You may notice the jaw dropping slightly and the back of the neck lengthening and widening. At the end of the exhale, it may feel like there is a compressed point in the middle of the throat. At the end of the exhale, hold the breath for a couple seconds, and as you inhale, try to subtly suck the breath upwards into the head, and watch or feel the upward sensations of the breath. Practice this for ten breaths.

See: Visualisation

Find a comfortable seated position with particular attention to a straight spine. Sit as though you were feeling particularly proud of yourself. We are going to learn *ujjai* breathing. This breath clears the throat and is known as the "victorious breath." It is characterised by the sound of the ocean. You make this sound by narrowing the passageway through the throat. Start by becoming aware of the breath in the nostrils. Watch or feel the breath as it enters through the nostrils and as it leaves the body through the nostrils. Now completely change your focus and imagine that the nostrils are closed, and intensify your attention to the throat. Imagine that your throat is now the nostrils. Try to narrow the airway in the throat, and create the ocean sound on both the inhale and the exhale. Make each in-breath and out-breath as long and slow as possible, and visualise the power and energy moving upwards into your head.

Continuing to create the ocean sound, focus more intensely on the in-breath and the upward movement of the energy. Feel yourself growing taller, stronger, and prouder with each breath. Continue for ten minutes.

Feel: The Vibration of *Udana*

The bumblebee breath—or *Bhramaree* breath—frees your mind of all that internal dialogue, enabling you to discover your voice of truth. This breathing exercise will help you sleep, improve concentration, and allow you to communicate at new profound levels. *Bhramaree* breath will encourage an extended exhalation, allowing you to let go of everything that is inside of you.

At bedtime, lay down on your bed with a pillow under your knees and another pillow under your head, and make sure your palms are facing up. Start to lengthen and slow down your breath for a few minutes. For the next ten minutes, you are going to inhale normally with your mouth closed and exhale while making the sound of a bumblebee. Keep your jaw and face relaxed and still. The sound comes from the throat, not the lips. Play with the pitch, and find the sound that feels more soothing and natural to you. It's that simple. At the end of the ten minutes, snuggle up and invite the blessing of deep, restful sleep.

Sing

In India, they love to sing and chant mantras. There is a science behind this that we will not go into here. However, singing opens the heart and makes you feel good. Get your favorite playlist and just sing along. Even better, go to a concert and sing your heart out. Don't worry if you think you can't sing. Who cares? Sing in the shower or the car or when walking the dog. The benefits of singing are cumulative. Try it daily! Watch and feel how your energy goes up. Most important of all, enjoy!

Eat: *Udana* Foods

Udana foods bring clarity to the mind and uplift the spirit. For example, consider fruit and nuts that grow in tall trees (bananas, cashew nuts, and brazil nuts); foods rich in omega-3 fatty acids (oily fish or seed alternatives like Udos oil); foods rich in selenium (brazil nuts, whole wheat, and tofu); foods that contain tryptophan (almonds, cottage cheese, and whole grains); foods rich in magnesium because it is uplifting, improves cognition, and reduces mental stress (brazil nuts, almonds, squash and pumpkin seeds, mackerel, avocado, and bananas), and *Brahmi*, an Ayurvedic herb associated with memory enhancement, quietening of the mind, and mental fatigue (available in most Ayurvedic stores and online).

Smells are very important for *udana*. Try an essential oil diffuser with uplifting oils like bergamot, geranium, grapefruit, lavender, and neroli.

Udana Affirmation

"I embrace and live my truth. I speak only the truth."

Reminder

- Remember that this is our first introduction to Lord Udana and we are working our way through each of the vayus, getting to know each one in turn.
- Take your time and try out all of the exercises as instructed.
- Write down your reflections and thoughts in your journal.
- This is the preparation for the five-week plan.
- You will find video resources for the exercises in this book at www.breathebettersleepbetter.co.uk
- You will find recipes for Udana food at www.breathebetter sleepbetter.co.uk

Chapter 9

Bringing It All Together, the Surrendered Breath

If you want more of me

If you try to grab me, you'll get less of me, not more of me

I'll come when I am ready

Trying to catch me for instant illumination won't work

You can't touch me with your hands, you can only feel me with your heart

Don't be impatient

The more you try to get hold of me and imprison me, the more I'll run away

When I see silence and surrender, I'll come closer

I'll sense the divine and look for union

The moment I see fear, I'll hide

I know I am elusive, like a wisp of divine incense, intangible, yet powerful, I promise, you'll get more of me by allowing me to be free

Let's dance together in the wind

- Anandi

The Journey So Far

We have come on a colorful journey through the five magnificent winds or *vayus*. We have looked at the many facets of each *vayu* – physical, scientific, psychological, subtle, and spiritual. We have located the area in the body and the directional force. Now is the time that we can start using the breath to heal every nook and cranny of our mind, body, and soul. Working with the breath in a profound way requires visualisation and intention to guide the breath. Without understanding how the breath works physically and subtly, it is impossible to utilise the breath to its full potential.

You now know that *prana* is the energy that brings oxygen and yummy goodness into your body. *Samana* digests it and separates the good from the bad. *Vyana* comes along and transports it to the farthest corners of the body, and *apana* disposes of all the waste. *Udana* then propels us forward in life with whatever resources the other four *vayus* have prepared for it. If you are not using the breath fully, your energy will be restricted, and the systems of the body cannot work as they are meant to, leaving you incomplete and severely lacking. However with abundant *prana*, a strong internal fire, free-flowing energy channels, and a good elimination system, you will bounce through life with vigor and enthusiasm.

My Research

This practice, the *Surrendered Breath*, is a result of my own research with surrender and breathing. I thought long and hard about the fact that, usually when we try to take a long, deep breath, we are orchestrating the whole thing with our mind. The realisation was that, if only we can get our mind out of the way, we could get more. I knew that working with breath calms the nervous system, not only from my teachers, but also from many of the research that is now published online. You will find a number of research articles showing the benefits of slow breathing on the parasympathetic nervous system on the National Center for Biotechnology Information website.[7]

When Guru-ji sent me away to practice belly breathing, part of me was disappointed because I thought I was capable of doing something more advanced than belly breathing, but that was my ego talking and an idea I was about to let go of like a hot potato. He showed me that it is the integrity of what you are doing that gives you the result. Of course advanced *pranayama* takes you forward with your journey and beyond, but as with anything, you need to create firm foundations first.

Doing this practice is actually much closer to the essence of yoga than jumping around in a yoga class with a fancy name. Simplicity is the key and "no extra drama," as Guru-ji would say.

The Surrendered Breath

I called this breath technique "the Surrendered Breath" because of the discovery in my own body. This approach to the breath is nothing new, but it is something that is often lost in Western yoga practice. Breathing fully requires an attitude of surrender and not force. Most people, if you told them to take a deep breath, would suck in their tummies and raise their shoulders. There is limited movement of the diaphragm downwards, and the capacity of the lungs to expand is restricted. I think it's something about the way we say "breathe in." It seems to imply that we move in the stomach.

By the same token, if you tell someone to breathe in and push out the belly, the breath becomes stifled and short because the person is focused on forcing out the belly instead of subtly expanding the rib cage and lengthening the breath. Allowing the belly to expand naturally, on the other hand, with the shape change caused by the contracting diaphragm is a completely different experience. Not until you surrender to the breathing mechanism and allow it to work as it should do you learn how to breathe properly. The Surrendered Breath allows your breathing apparatus to work as it is supposed to. Your only part in this is to surrender so your body can open the door to the *pranic* vital force.

In life, we aim to control everything in order to have more, but if we try to control this process, we will get less and not more. Think surrender, allow, and soften! Your in-breath and out-breath will flow without effort, and your body will fill with *prana*, if you let it! The following practice requires you to surrender and not to intellectualise the process. Be patient with yourself. All yogic practices are called "practice" for a reason. The dictionary definition of practice is "to do" or "perform" (something) repeatedly in order to acquire or polish a skill, implying you have to do it to have any level of success. Just remember, the more trying you do, the more difficult it will be.

My Experiment

Let me take you back for a moment, to the day Guru-ji gave me this practice. At the time, I was feeling that, after all these years of practice, something was still missing. I was looking to Guru-ji for guidance and inspiration. Somehow he always knows what I am talking about, even if I am not explaining myself very well. He told me I had to do this practice for at least thirty days and report back to him. The conversation finished, and I prepared myself to follow the instructions and organise my usual ritual to accommodate this new piece.

The following day, I started with my usual practice. Then I snuggled myself up on my yoga mat with a cushion under my knees and a number of blankets. I started by just watching and observing the breath and, in particular, breathing into my belly. I did not intend to do anything different. I just did as I was instructed. I was particularly relaxed that day, and surrendering myself to the earth seemed easy. After about five minutes, my attention somehow intensified on the pause between the inhale and the exhale, especially at the end of the exhale. I did not try to intellectualise it. I noticed and watched. I started enjoying all the sensations at the point where the inhale became the exhale and the exhale became the inhale. I found it fascinating how the body magically knows what to do.

I continued to surrender myself to the earth until I was somewhere between the waking and sleeping state of consciousness. In this state, everything is soft. You feel as if you can't move, but you could if you really wanted to. In hypnosis, they call this the "hypnogogic state." In yoga, we call it *Yoga Nidra*. It is a blissful state, allowing deep physical and mental rest. The breathing automatically changes. It becomes deeper and more profound.

As I went deeper into that state, I started allowing my body to take the breath when it was ready instead of me consciously trying to breathe deeply. As I continued, on the next exhale, I breathed out the last drop of air, and I waited a bit longer, resisting the temptation to grapple, panic, and snatch for the next breath for fear of death. There was a huge temptation for my mind to take over, and of course, I failed to resist it. As my mind jumped in, I knew that, if only I had the patience to wait, something marvelous would happen.

I kept going with my practice, just focusing intensely on my belly and doing my utmost not to interfere with the breath. What started to happen was so beautiful. As I lay there softening the stiffness and letting of the incessant desire to control everything, I felt the door to *prana* open. When you normally take a deep breath, you imagine it starts in the nose. This was different. It was as though I was no longer the one doing the breathing. Divine breath was taking over my body. Energy started to rise at the point of my pubic bone and slowly infuse the lower belly. It was as though every single cell of my internal organs was breathing *prana*. The breath started to rise and rise and rise through the middle of my body and then head to the upper chest, to what felt like my shoulder blades. It kept coming, even though intellectually I did not think there was any more space for breath as my lungs felt full. This breath was not a normal breath. It was something else.

As it reached my shoulder blades, the rest of my body continued to expand. I was overflowing with *prana* until another pause came and a change of direction was imminent.

I was again tempted to let it all out immediately, but I waited for a moment for my body to become ready to release the breath and take away that which I no longer needed. The breath left my body in a long stream of emotions, sensations, and, above all, huge relief. It felt like all the stuff that did not serve me was beginning to liquefy and dissolve, as if I had somehow lost weight, but emotional weight, not physical weight. It was an almighty liberation and a sense of peace.

I then waited for the next breath, and in anticipation I tried to repeat the same experience with my intellect. The breath froze, and I felt like I couldn't breathe. I realised straight away that the mind wanted more and crudely tried to grasp as it stifled and suffocated the in-breath. There was the lesson. Grabbing and grasping for fear of scarcity blocks the flow of energy, whatever you are grasping for.

Pranayama is all about expansion and guidance of *prana* rather than control. It was truly an enlightening moment and something that took me over ten years of yoga practice to discover. It was as though Guru-ji intuitively knew the only way I would learn how to breathe was by sending me off to do a simple breathing exercise. This is the way you learn from a guru, not by sitting and listening, but by going away and doing exactly what he says. You can learn principles, facts, and mountains of philosophy. You can have bookshelves brimming with guides and teachings on yoga. If you are impatient and not prepared to start at the beginning and you try to run before you can walk, you will miss the message of yoga altogether. One might imagine that this book is for beginners, which was my intention at the outset. But I have now realised that, like me, many yoga practitioners would learn important lessons by going back to the very essence of breathing, doing this practice, and having this experience. Only from here can you truly appreciate more advanced breathing techniques.

As I continued with this practice, I increased the time as directed to forty minutes a session. I also started timing the length of a breath guided by the mind versus the length of a fully surrendered breath. To my complete surprise, the guided breath lasted fifteen to twenty seconds, but the surrendered breath lasted forty-five to fifty seconds. This was just the beginning of the appreciation of a glorious daily *pranic* bath, one I am excited to share with you.

Making Space for the Breath

The Surrendered Breath

Surrender my love

I want to merge with you

Why won't you let me in?

I only want to love you

but your door is closed

I just want to give you life, I don't need anything from you

I want to nourish you

Don't separate yourself from me

I want to be with you

Don't you love me?

Why are you so intent on resisting my love?

Are you worried that if you surrender to me, you'll loose control?

Surrender, and I promise to love you, don't be afraid.

Now, feel me whispering to you, if you listen, just listen, you'll hear my truth

I'll take you to a place where we can sing, dance and become divinely one

I love you.

- Anandi

Breath Liberation Practice

Yoga postures are designed precisely for making space in the body and allowing room for the breathing process. I have created this practice specifically for increasing the capacity for volume by mobilising the upper chest and back through my own experimentation and working with amazing teachers like Leslie Kaminoff and Yogi Vishvketu. The average lung capacity in an adult male is six liters of air,[6] of which only a small amount is used during normal breathing. Some free divers can increase their lung capacity up to fifteen liters. For this to happen, the thoracic cavity would need to be completely free and unrestricted. Tight muscles and poor posture needs to be corrected. Even if we could tap into some of the potential the breath has to offer, we would feel more alive.

These exercises are simple and easy to do. The whole practice will take you just thirty minutes. If you make the breath liberation practice part of your daily routine for at least thirty days, you will soon start noticing that you are able to lengthen your breath and expand your chest with ease.

Note: You will find video resources for these exercises at www.breathe bettersleepbetter.co.uk

Cat Cow

Objective: Wakes up and mobilises the spine and upper back

How to: Come into a table position with the knees hip-width apart, the fingers spread out, and hands aligned with the shoulders. Take an inhale and exhale here. On the next inhale, look up and imagine a golden cord running through the navel that is pulling your navel down towards the earth. On the exhale, tuck the chin back toward the chest, and imagine that golden cord is pulling the navel towards the heavens. Round the spine as much as possible, especially the upper spine. Now close your eyes and continue the inhale and exhale with the movement. Continue for twenty breaths.

Magic Chest Opener

Objective: Lifts the sternum and opens thoracic cavity

How to: Sit on a chair or cross-legged on a cushion. If you are sitting on a cushion, make sure your knees are slightly lower than your hips to stop your spine from collapsing. Bring your hands to the side of your body and turn the palms so they are facing out. Inhale, raise arms up at the side of the body, hold the breath in, bring down the arms without moving your shoulders or dropping the sternum, and then exhale, maintaining the new more open posture. Inhale fully; exhale fully. Continue for ten sets.

Shoulder Opening

Objective: Mobilises and relaxes the shoulder and chest muscles

How to: From a seated position on a chair or sitting on a cushion, keep your back straight and your arms relaxed down the side of your body. (If on a cushion, make sure your knees are slightly lower than your hips.) Inhale, gently look upwards, externally rotate the arms, and squeeze the shoulder blades. As you exhale, bring the chin back down to the collarbone, internally rotate the shoulders forward, and squeeze the chest. Continue for twenty breaths.

Lateral Side Bend

Objective: Stretches the side ribs

How to: If sitting in an armchair, put your right arm on the arm of the chair, inhale, and raise your left arm, rotating the arm internally so the palm of the hand faces inwards. And reach the left arm over towards the right side. Keep both sitting bones with contact on the chair. Keep the length in the rib cage so you are not collapsing into the kidney area. Take three breaths here. Inhale, come back up, and exhale. Release the arm back down to the side. Repeat the other side. Continue for five sets.

If sitting on a yoga mat, it's exactly the same process. You may have the supporting elbow or hand on the ground.

The Doorway Stretch

Objective: Stretches the pectoral muscles, a marvelous chest-opening experience

How to: Stand in a doorway with your feet about six inches back from the doorway, and put both hands on either side of the door, level with the chest, and ease your weight forward. Take ten to fifteen breaths here.

The Thumb-Clasp Chest Opener

Objective: Expands the chest and the lungs

How to: Clasp the thumbs behind your back with your arms as straight as possible. As you inhale, bend your elbows, and as you exhale, straighten your arms and ease up your arms. Your shoulders will roll back, and your chest will open. Take five breaths here.

Katichakrasasana

Objective: Expands the chest and mobilises the upper spine

How to: Stand with the feet hip-width apart or a bit farther. Keep feet parallel even when you are twisting. Careful not to sway back, keep the tailbone tucked down towards the earth. Keep the muscles in your legs and tummy engaged. Inhale. Raise the arms out to shoulder height with the palms facing upwards. Exhale and twist to the right-hand side, keeping the chest open and twisting through the ankles, knees, hips, waist, and all the way up the spine to the neck. Look over the right shoulder, as far as is comfortable for your neck. Try to keep the arms at 180 degrees. Take five breaths here. Inhale, come back to the centre, exhale, and float the arms down. Repeat the other side.

The Eye Gaze

Objective: Mobilises the upper spine and opens the chest

How to: By fixing the eyes on the hands and limiting the movement of the eyeballs as you move the hands and follow them with your gaze, you will be amazed at which parts of your body actually move. Stand with your feet hip-width apart. Clasp the hands together in front of you with the index finger on both hands pointing outwards. Look down at your index fingers, and keep your gaze fixed on the fingers. Start moving your hands out to the left, upwards, and sidewards. And create a circle around to the left. Just play with the moving hands, but keep your gaze on the fingers. Do the same from the right side. Continue for one minute.

Finger Walking

Objective: Opens the chest

How to: Stand about a foot away from the wall. Bring your hand up on to the wall in a straight line, and start walking your fingers up the wall. You will feel a wonderful stretch of the side chest. Once you have reached the maximum that your body is comfortable with, walk your fingers backwards and upwards, and feel the top front chest open.

Mountain Brook Pose

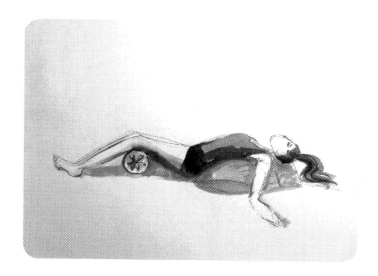

Objective: Opens the chest and makes space for the breath

How to: You will need to experiment with the amount of support you have under your back. The absolute key is comfort. If you feel that your back is arched, you need to have less underneath your back. Gather together two or three blankets, and get a soft cushion for under your head and neck and a bolster for under your knees. Sit on the floor on a yoga mat in front of a blanket folded into two or three. Have it longways. Have the cushion ready to put under your head and neck and the bolster for under your knees. Lay back and snuggle down onto the support under your back. Have the top line of the blanket in alignment with your armpits so your chest lifts and opens. It is vital that you take the time to get comfortable. Your lower back should never feel uncomfortable. Start by staying for a couple minutes, and then build up to five minutes. To come out, ease your elbows and hands down, and push yourself off the props. Then lay back down without the props, and hug your knees.

Chapter 11

The Surrendered Breath Practices

Kumbhaka
"At the end of the exhale,
Breath surrenders to quietude.
For a moment you hang in the balance—
Suspended
In the fertile spaciousness
That is the source of breath.
At the end of the inhale,
Filled with the song of the breath,
There is a moment when you are simply
Holding the tender mystery.
In these interludes,
Experience opens into exquisite vastness
With no beginning and no end.
Embrace this infinity without reservation.
You are its vessel"

—Lorin Roche, *The Radiance Sutras*

This is the wonderful moment when you bring everything together
that you have learned so far. We have seen that there is a fundamental

difference between guiding and controlling the breath. If you try to control the breath, it will shorten. And if you surrender the breath, it will lengthen. We can now appreciate that the breath is not just oxygen. It carries with it the life force energy of *prana*, which has different energetic aspects to it. We can now find, appreciate, and expand each of these subtle aspects of the *vayus*. We are able to use the whole of the breathing apparatus and have an understanding of how it all works. We have studied the various practices for each *vayu*. Now we are ready to practice and appreciate the subtle differences in breathing through the Surrendered Breath practices.

Preparing Your Yoga Space

None of the practices in this book can be rushed, and you need to think about where you will be doing your practice and create an appropriate space for yourself. Preparation is very much a part of the process. Honoring it with all of your intention will deepen your connection to it. Everyone will have a different way of creating the perfect nurturing space, so it's important to find whatever makes you feel comfortable, relaxed, and nurtured. Appealing to the senses is a powerful way of connecting and uplifting the spirit.

A calming and relaxing environment appeals to the visual sense. Think for a moment about how you feel when you step into a temple with beautiful imagery, flowers, and soothing colors. It usually has a calming effect on our state of being, and we often feel spiritually motivated by simply being in that energy. You could create an altar with a deity or an image of someone that inspires you to encourage a 100 per cent participation from your heart. Our surroundings have a profound effect on our consciousness, and we can easily change them with a little awareness.

Our spirit is also easily touched through the sense of hearing. Soft, relaxing music can change our mood and will have a peaceful effect on our consciousness. Find some music that evokes an inner sense of peace and have that just quietly playing in the background.

The skin responds to the sense of touch. Having soft, sumptuous, even cashmere blankets to wrap yourself up in will send you to heaven. As you relax, your body temperature will go down. You may feel cold, so it's important to make sure you feel warm. The sense of smell is a vital trigger towards your stillness and is not to be underestimated. Light your favorite candle or incense, and it will start transporting you to stillness.

If you don't have a dedicated space in your home for your practice, have a beautiful box that you can keep everything in so you only have to open the container and prepare rather than running around looking for everything. You will need a yoga mat and a cushion for under your knees, preferably a soft bolster or pillow, and a cushion or pillow for under your head. You will need a timer so you don't have to keep looking at the clock. Your blankets should be kept sacred for your practice only. You will either need to have read the script and rehearsed the practice a number of times so you know what you are doing or download *The Surrendered Breath* audio from www.breathebettersleepbetter.co.uk.

Make the practice a ritualistic affair as you prepare your space. Put a "do not disturb notice" out to the rest of the household. Turn off your mobile and your computer as you certainly do not want to be hearing the ding of incoming emails to keep you from melting away into the great unknown. To get the most out of this ritual, you need to mentally close the door on the outside world to open the door to your inside world. A slightly darkened room will also help the relaxation process.

Make sure you do not do your practice on a full stomach. A busy digestive system will prevent you from relaxing and working with the breath fully.

My Ritual

I practice early in the morning just before sunrise. I find this is the best time. As the sun rises, so does the mental chatter in my mind. I always wear my warm, comfortable yoga clothes and a light-colored cashmere pashmina for my practice. (Light colors are uplifting for spiritual practice.) These are my physical "sense of feel" things that instantly connect me to my inner journey. I never wear shoes in my yoga room, as it symbolises leaving my mental stuff outside a sacred space.

I light a candle on my altar where I have flowers. I also have my favorite deity Shiva, who epitomises the destruction of the ego and makes way for the true self, and a photo of my Guru-ji. I honor the spirit of Shiva and Guru-ji. Then I go and sit on my mat and start my practice.

Your Turn

This practice requires you to be completely relaxed. Running in from work, lying down, and trying to rush surrendering yourself to the earth won't work. Your heart rate will be racing, your breath will be shallow, and your mind will be all over the place. First you have to unravel yourself in order to start the process. Make sure you follow the preparation guidelines before your practice.

Unravel Yourself First with "Legs Up the Wall"

I recommend Legs Up the Wall to nearly everyone, as it has such a heavenly, rejuvenating power and will bring you back down to earth from your running and rushing. This yoga pose's name is *Viparita*

Karani, which is often translated as "inverted lake." It is a marvelous preparation to quiet everything down. That includes your mind and your nervous and circulatory systems. It is also wondrous for tired legs.

For the duration of this pose, you are doing nothing but natural breathing and, on each exhale, sighing and letting it all go. You can make a noise as you sigh or simply let go in silence. Enjoy and savor not doing and just being. Stress and tiredness will disappear into the earth. Practice this for five to ten minutes before the Surrendered Breath practice.

How to Do It

Getting There

- Sit on the floor with one shoulder near the wall, and make sure your thighs are parallel to the wall.

- Let yourself down onto your shoulder.

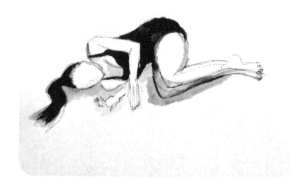

- Swing your legs up onto the wall.

Coming Out

- Bend your knees towards your chest.

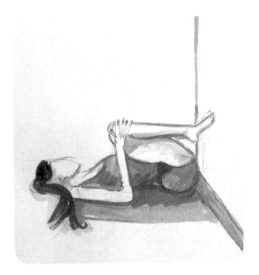

- Roll over to your right side.

- Gently bring yourself up with the help of your hands.

Cautions and Adjustments

- Make sure your lower back is supported and not arched. If it is, just ease yourself off the wall so your lower back is in contact with the floor. You can add a blanket under your hips or a bolster to support the back.
- If your hamstrings are tight or your knees are uncomfortable, simply move out from the wall about one-third of a metre, bend your legs, and rest your feet on the wall.

Contraindications include heart and neck problems, menstruation, and pregnancy. Always check with your health-care advisor first.

The Surrendered Breath Practices Explained

The *Pranic Bath*

We have seen how the lungs work and the resulting shape change of the diaphragm when you breathe using your lungs in their entirety. On the in-breath, the diaphragm contracts, and the stomach expands as it facilitates the expansion of the thoracic cavity. During the *pranic* bath, you will feel *prana* going beyond your lungs, as if the whole of your being is filling with energy. This is so much more than air. When you exhale, you will feel an entire release and a wave of weightlessness.

Taking this *pranic* bath will relax you in a way that nothing else can. Oxygen, nutrients, and hormones will get to where they are needed instead of leaving certain areas of the body "*prana* famished." One area of particular importance relating to stress and sleep is the brain. Your brain uses about three times as much oxygen as your muscles, and oxygen-starved brain cells wither and die very quickly. Your brain needs oxygen for the oxidation process, and it is the catalyst for producing energy and life. The least you can do for our treasured body and mind is learn how to breathe. You don't even have to go to the gym for that!

The Cleansing Breath Practice

As we know, *apana* is our cleansing breath, and *samana* is the force of digestion and transformation. In the cleansing breath practice, we are stoking the fire of *samana* and energising *apana*.

Samana needs two things to function: the right kind of fuel and the energy to burn brightly. *Apana* also needs two things to function properly: well-digested food and the energy to move it through the intestines. In this cleansing breath practice, we supply the energy to both *samana* and *apana* to digest and transform the fuel we give our body and rid ourselves of waste and toxins, the two fundamentals of a healthy body and a tranquil mind.

Individual *Vayu* Consciousness

In this practice we are going to get a feel for each individual directional force by intensifying our awareness at the trigger points we found in the discovery section. Focusing on each *vayu* will awaken, activate, and boost its potential power in the dance of the *vayus*.

The *Vayu Nidra*

Nidra is the Sanskrit word for sleep. If you don't have my yoga sleep audio, I recommend you try it, as it will help you understand the value of true relaxation and it is a great way to start the Surrendered Breath practice. In *Yoga Nidra*, you enter a state of complete physical and mental relaxation where you are floating between the sleeping and waking states of consciousness. You are neither asleep nor awake in the normal sense of the word. In *Vayu Nidra*, you are relaxing and opening all of the associated parts of the subtle energy system of each directional force. Because your body and the breathing apparatus is completely relaxed, *vayu* can flow with fluidity and freedom. Through the various Surrendered Breath practices, you will be in a state of *nidra*, and with a little subtle attention, you will start feeling the energy of all the *vayus* working simultaneously. It gives you an extraordinary sense of lightness and the sensation of floating. All the physical weight of the body melts into the earth, and the senses will be heightened to the subtle *vayu* energy. Through this practice, you will start to experience a new kind of stillness, peace, and joy.

Savasana

The word *savasana* means "corpse pose," and it allows for the integration of your practice. The work we are doing has a stimulating and balancing effect on the systems of the body, and you need to give yourself this time to absorb the benefits. *Savasana* has a very grounding effect on the body, mind, and spirit, and it is an excellent transition between physical practice and meditation. You will see I have started the practices section below with *savasana*, as you will need to know what that is first to enable you to follow the instructions for the Surrendered Breath.

The Practices

The ideal way to do these practices is to download the Surrendered Breath audio and step by step guide from www.breathebettersleepbetter. co.uk. Then you can simply relax, and I will guide you. If not, you will need to read the script several times so you know what you are doing before you start.

You can either do the Surrendered Breath short practice, which consists of the *pranic* bath and *savasana*, or the long practice, which consists of the *pranic* bath, the cleansing breath, individual *vayu* consciousness practice, *Vayu Nidra*, and *savasana*.

The *Pranic* Bath: Practice

Get yourself in a comfortable position on your back, and make sure you have a cushion under your head and your body is warm and supported. You should feel heavenly and super comfortable. Now you are ready to start your *pranic* bath. Each and every cell of your body will get bathed in nourishing *prana*.

Simply observe the breath. Watch, feel, and notice as the breath enters and leaves the body. Notice the sensations as the body moves internally and externally with the in-breath and the out-breath. Now focus on your belly, and observe the rise and fall with the in-breath and the out-breath. Allow yourself to relax, melt, and soften.

Let your body breathe naturally. Trust that your body will take the breath without you having to reach for it. Don't try to force the breath in any way. Just be with it as it arises. Relax and just feel the breath. You are not breathing the breath; the breath is breathing you. Allow yourself to surrender enough so you can feel as though you are being breathed by divine breath.

Start noticing the exchange of direction internally at the moment the out-breath becomes the in-breath and the in-breath becomes the out-breath. Watch and notice the pause between the in-breath and the out-breath. Just watch and become even more aware of this pause.

Now slightly increase that pause at the end of the out-breath by maybe one second. Just imagine you are giving the subtle energy more time to change direction. You are not holding your breath. You are simply waiting. Stay with that slight extra pause. Watch, feel, and notice the sensations as the breath spontaneously enters the body on the inhale. Allow the body to release the breath when it is ready, like a wave crashing to the shore as the breath leaves on the exhale. Do not at any time try to breath in or out. Just allow the door of the breath to open and close, and completely surrender yourself to the earth.

Now increase the pause at the end of the out-breath by another one or two seconds, and during that pause, release and dissolve the body into the earth. You are simply waiting; you are not holding the breath. Surrender yourself to the earth and do nothing.

As you relax, feel as if you are dissolving your body, and focus on relaxing everything from the pubic bone downwards. At the end of the out-breath, don't force. Just completely let go and watch the downward sensation of the energy in the lower belly as the body starts to take the breath. Imagine all the internal organs relaxing as the downward force eases the energy towards the earth, but at the same time, the upward forces start to rise the energy through the body. Stay focused on this sensation as the breath enters the body. If you remain patient, the energetic breath will keep coming right up into your shoulder blades and continue to the crown of the head and beyond. Stay focused on this sensation as the energy and breath seeps through the body. Keep observing this for a few minutes. If you lose the rhythm of surrender, take a normal breath and start again.

Now bring your attention to the upper body. Be careful not to lose the complete relaxation of the lower body. Become aware of the rising, forward direction of the chest as the breath fills the thoracic cavity, and notice how the chest moves down towards the mid-belly on the out-breath.

Bring your attention back to the pause between the out-breath and in-breath. Increase the pause again by a second or two. Release and surrender the body more fully. Watch the two forces of *prana* and *apana* bring the breath into the body, and push the breath out of the body like a beautiful synchronised dance. *Prana* and *apana* move towards each other and away from each other without ever losing contact. Two energies, separate but yet still entwined, move in glorious unity, complementing each move with another and basking in union in the flames of *samana*. Continue observing this for a few minutes.

Now relax the skin around the body. Imagine that there are no boundaries and you become one with the environment. Maintain the attitude of complete surrender. Envision you are breathing in synchronicity with the universe, watching, feeling, and allowing the universal breath to lovingly massage you from the inside. Feel the blissful sensations as you allow your body to fill with *prana*. Savor every single divine moment. (If you are doing the short practice, continue for ten minutes and then release into *savasana*.)

Savasana (Integration Practice)

Completely release your attention from the breath. Allow any sensations to melt away. Permit yourself to be in the state of being. Float in the bliss from the practice, and savor each and every moment. Be in this moment. Stay here for ten minutes.

The Cleansing Breath Practice

Start this practice with a ten-minute *pranic* bath. We will now start guiding the purifying, cleansing breath to detoxify your whole system. Continue to relax and dissolve the body, focusing in particular on relaxing everything from the pubic bone downwards. At the end of the out-breath, don't force. Just completely let go, and as the in-breath enters the body, watch the downward sensation of the energy in the lower belly. As the breath and energy continues to seep into the mid-belly, watch, sense, feel, or imagine the inward moving force at the navel. On each inhale, imagine all the internal organs relaxing, as the downward force of *apana* eases the energy towards the earth, together with the energy of *samana* as it works its way inwards towards the centre of your belly. Keep your attention on these two forces for the whole of the in-breath. There will also be some expansion of the thoracic cavity as the lungs take in the air, but the focus is on the subtle energy in the lower and mid-belly. Feel the internal organs become saturated with *prana*: the stomach, liver, gallbladder, pancreas, and intestines, the complete digestive system. When the body releases the breath, feel the relief that goes with the out-breath as it takes with it emotions and old stuff that is no longer serving you.

Individual *Vayu* Consciousness: The Practice

We will now start bringing our awareness to each individual *vayu*, awakening and boosting their power. As you continue the surrendering of the breath, you will start to notice the different directional forces of the breath by focusing and intensifying your attention on each *vayu*.

Return your attention now to all the sensations of the breathing body. Notice once again the exchange of direction internally at the moment the out-breath becomes the in-breath and the in-breath becomes the out-breath. Watch the pause between them. Continue for a few moments.

We will start with *apana*, the detoxifying downward force. Take a long, deep inhale, and exhale into the trigger point of *apana*, the anus. You may feel at the end of the exhale that the anus pulls up as you become completely empty. When your body is ready, completely surrender your lower belly. You may notice the downward force sensations in the lower belly as the body takes the breath. As your lower belly expands, imagine all your internal organs coming to life as they fill with life force energy. And as you exhale let go, let go, let go. Repeat and continue for ten breaths. Release your attention from *apana*, and continue to breathe using the Surrendered Breath technique for a few moments.

We will now move to *samana*, the digestive inward force that moves towards the centre of the human being. It keeps your internal fire energised and gives you balance and equilibrium. Now bring your attention to the centre of your body. Take a long, deep inhale and exhale into the trigger point, four fingers below the belly button, until you are completely empty. You may notice this area becoming more compact. When your body is ready, guide the energy into the mid-belly. Allow the belly to fill from all sides.

You may notice that, even though you are expanding as you inhale, a force is pulling in towards the centre If you can't feel it, imagine a concentration of energy in your mid-belly. Intensify any sensations, and visualise a fire crackling, transforming, and manifesting. Imagine the heat and the freedom as *samana* goes to work. Repeat and continue for ten breaths. Release your attention from the *samana vayu* area of the body, and continue to breathe using the Surrendered Breath technique for a few moments.

Now bring your attention to *prana*, the forward-moving energy that enables us to live and move as human beings. Bring your attention to the chest, watch, feel, and notice the movement of the chest. Observe how the chest moves upwards and outwards as you inhale. Take a long, deep breath, and as you exhale, exhale into the trigger point at the sternum in the same way you did in the discovery exercise. When you are completely empty, you may feel that the area of the trigger point feels compact. Inhale into the upper chest, expanding the chest front, back, and sides. Intensify the sensations of the incoming life force and sensations of expansion. Repeat and continue for five minutes. Release your attention from the *prana vayu* area of the body, and continue to breathe using the Surrendered Breath technique for a few moments.

We will now move our attention upwards to *udana*, the creative force that gives us the power to express ourselves in the physical world. Take a long, deep inhale, and exhale into the dip in the throat area until you are empty. Again you may feel this area becoming compact and the back of the neck lengthen slightly. When you are ready, inhale, drawing the energy into the head. You may feel the *udana* drawing upwards or even going out of the crown of your head. You might also feel a new lightness in the head as your attention moves into space. Repeat and continue for ten breaths. Release your attention from the *udana*, and continue to breathe using the Surrendered Breath technique for a few moments.

We will now move to *vyana*, the ever-present circulatory force. Move your attention to the boundaries of the body. Take a long, deep inhale, and exhale into the centre of your body until you are completely empty. When your body is ready to inhale, allow the body to take the breath, and notice the energy moving outwards from your core, through the skin, and beyond. You may notice the tingling of the skin as you imagine you are inhaling and exhaling through the skin. Breathe in and out through every pore of the skin, imagining that your whole body is one entity rather than individual parts. Repeat and continue for ten breaths. Release your attention from *vyana*, and continue to breathe using the Surrendered Breath technique for a few moments.

Completely release any isolated awareness, and release your whole being to the earth and float. If your mind wanders off, keep bringing it back to the breath. Stay there for five minutes.

The *Vayu Nidra* Practice

We will now let go of the physical body and focus on breathing the subtle body. Stay completely relaxed as you continue to surrender your breath. We are now going to get a sense of all the five divine majestic winds interacting with each other in the same way as the five elements work together in nature. You will feel the joy of the subtle communication of these great forces moving like the waves of a beautiful ocean. The breath is like the crescendo of water in the ocean as it rises, getting ready to crash to the shore and then pulling back again into the ocean. It's an effortless waxing and waning of different spiritual powers. Riding the wave of the breath is like moving with the freedom of the ocean.

Now as you inhale, the body starts its expansion from the pubic bone. See if you can get a sensation of all the five forces moving together simultaneously as the body starts to expand with the in-breath. Feel the dance of *prana* and *apana* and, at the same time, the inward force of *samana*, the expanding sensations of *vyana*, and the upward force of *udana*. Sense the *vayus* moving as one unit north, south, east, and west, while at the same time drawing inwards to the central core of the body. Focus on the synchronicity of the five winds ebbing and flowing as you surrender and allow your body to be breathed by divine breath. Release your physical form, and join the dance.

Feel the liberating sensations as the five winds move your body freely without physical restriction from your controlling mind. Imagine you have fallen through the hard mental layers and are resting in the blissful core of your being. This bliss is called *anand*. Stay with these sensations for ten minutes.

Savasana

Now completely release your attention from the breath. Allow any sensations to melt away. Just allow yourself to be in the state of being. Float in the bliss from the practice, and savor each and every moment. Be in this moment. Stay here for five minutes.

Now slowly start to prepare to return to your body. Bring your attention to your physical body and where it meets with the earth. Make small movements with your hands and your feet, and move your head from side to side. Slowly roll over onto your right side and help yourself up with your hands.

You may feel a bit groggy straight after the practice. Take a shower, give yourself a spritz of something yummy, and make a green juice. Whatever you have, make it nutritious. I promise you, after about an hour, you will start to feel marvelous.

> *"The breath is the most powerful healing tool to the human being"*
>
> -Yogi Vishvketu

Record Your Discoveries

Make sure you are recording your journey through the five winds in your journal. As you work through this program, writing down any sensations, physical or emotional, will help you get clarity on your thoughts and feelings and get you in touch with your internal world. It will also help you recognise toxic situations that keep coming up and help you find solutions to resolve them. When feelings become intense, journaling diffuses emotions and helps open your mind to different perspectives so your inner learning will become more profound.

Chapter 12

The Five-Week Plan

"In the breath, the soul finds an opportunity to speak.
Images or intuition, poetry or wordless wisdom come and
go, no effort but to breathe and listen"

—Donna Faulds

Make Sure You Are Ready

Before you start this program, it is paramount that you have prepared yourself by following the guidance on how to get the best out of this book, which is at the beginning. Have you read the whole book to orientate yourself with the concepts and experimented with the practices? If you haven't, you'll need to resist the temptation to go directly into the five-week program and instead take yourself back to the beginning so you get the maximum benefit.

Take the Time to Create Space for Your Practice

Time is an issue for most people. We tend to spend most of it split between the things that simply have to get done for our life to function and stuff that wastes our time, like surfing the Internet and constantly checking our email and Facebook. The important life-giving things that improve the quality of your life are usually last on the list. The only way you are going to make taking the time to look after yourself an integral part of your day is to start prioritising things differently.

How to Sustain Your Practice

The key is to create rhythm and a routine. Unfortunately there is no magical way of achieving this, and no one can do your practice for you. Make your rhythm steady and keep rededicating yourself to your practice. Everyone starts with great enthusiasm, but the real work starts when one has to find the inner discipline to continue. It's too easy to allow your daily busyness with urgent matters to get in the way. Don't try to do it all at once, and make sure you follow all the recommendations. The danger of rushing and doing too much is that you will likely be setting yourself up for failure and give yourself an excellent excuse to give up.

If you have set up your new priorities and decide that your health and well-being is one of them, you are 75 per cent there. It all starts with the intention. Enlisting an accountability partner is a great way of maintaining motivation and keeping your commitments towards yourself or kick-starting the process on a retreat where you are not going to get caught up in your usual time-wasting activities.

The Five-Week Plan

This five-week plan is designed to help you find your way around the subtle aspects of the breath. Provided you follow the instructions, you will learn how to use the breath for healing, releasing stress, detoxifying the body, and rediscovering deep, profound sleep. Your breathing will never be the same again after this process. It will become alive, multifaceted, and a way for you to connect to the inner spirit.

Don't forget to record your discoveries on this journey, and write your reflections and things that are coming up for you during the practice at the end of each day. Once you have completed the five-week program, looking back at your journal will be extremely useful as you will be able to see clearly just how far you have come, and it will encourage you to continue your journey and even share it with others.

Let's Get the Plan Started

Decide what time of day you are able to dedicate to your practice. This needs to be the same time every day. You will need about forty-five minutes of quiet, undisturbed time. Morning is best, but if you can't manage morning, you can do it at bedtime, but make sure it is not on a full stomach. Be serious about the recommended visualisations and affirmations. They are very much part of the practice.

You may notice that the discover, feel, and visualisation practices are not always in the same order for the five-week plan as they are in the presentation part of this book. This is because, in the context of a practice as opposed to the discovery lessons we have been doing as we worked through the *vayus*, they may need to be in a different order. You may also notice that all the practices start with Legs Up the Wall (chapter xxxxx), followed by *Kapalabhati Kriya* (chapter xxxxx). Legs Up the Wall will get you in the right state mentally and physically, and *Kapalabhati Kriya* cleanses the energy channels, clears the mind, and makes way for the practice.

Important Note

You will find video resources for the exercises at www.breathebetter sleepbetter.co.uk

Week 1: Getting Acquainted, *Prana* Vayu

This is the *prana vayu* week. As you have seen, *prana* is the essence, the life force that drives all of life on this planet. Finding the source in your own body and making the space for the breath are the very first steps. Remember the significance of the word *pranayama*, which means expansion and guidance of *prana*. This week we will be doing just that.

Prepare Yourself

- Read the chapter on *prana vayu* again and answer the "Let's Check In" questions.
- Note your weak points, and resolve to do at least one action this week to get more connected to *prana*.
- Write your *pranic*-expanding goal.
- Get more *prana*-rich foods. Write down the changes you are going to make to your diet this week.

Seven-Day *Prana Vayu* Daily Practice

	Page
During the Day	
Visualisation—*prana* channeling—ten breaths five times per day: before breakfast, before lunch, mid-afternoon, before dinner, and before bed	42
Prana affirmation—five minutes three times per day: before breakfast, before lunch, and before dinner	43
Practice	
Legs Up the Wall—five minutes	127
Kapalabhati Kriya—twenty seconds for two rounds	87

Breath liberation exercises	113
Feel hands breathing—three rounds of ten breaths	42
Discover *prana*—three rounds of ten breaths	41
Anuloma Viloma—eleven rounds	24
Pranic bath—ten minutes	134
Rest quietly for ten minutes in *savasana*	136

Week 2: Getting Acquainted with *Samana Vayu*

This is the *samana vayu* week. You have started making space for the breath and have taken steps to bring in more *prana*. Paying attention to your food and bringing more energy into the digestive system will stoke the internal fire.

Prepare Yourself

- Read the chapter on *samana vayu* again and answer the "Let's Check In" questions.
- Note your weak points and resolve to do at least one action this week to get more connected to *samana*.
- Write your *samana*-expanding goal.
- Get more *samana*-rich foods. Write down the changes you are going to make to your diet this week.

Seven-Day *Samana Vayu* Daily Practice

	Page
Samana affirmation—five minutes three times per day: before breakfast, before lunch, and before dinner	59
Practice	
Legs Up the Wall—five minutes	127
Kapalabhati Kriya—thirty seconds for two rounds	87
Breath liberation exercises	113
Discover *samana*—three rounds of ten breaths	57
Feel: sun breathing—five minutes Sun breathing should be done in the morning.	58
Visualisation—fire in your belly breathing exercise—five minutes	58
Cleansing breath practice—ten minutes	132
Rest quietly for ten minutes in *savasana*	136

Week 3: Getting Acquainted with *Vyana Vayu*

This is your *vyana* week. We are going to get energy moving and flowing. It's time to open your mind, explore, and then cut off the chains that keep you small. Grow, reach, and expand to the infinite realms of *vyana vayu*.

Prepare Yourself

- Read the chapter on *vyana vayu* again and answer the "Let's Check In" questions.

- Note your weak points and resolve to take at least one action this week to get more connected to *vyana*.
- Write your *vyana*-expanding goal.
- Get more *vyana*-rich foods. Write down the changes you are going to make to your diet this week.

Seven-Day *Vyana Vayu* Daily Practice

	Page
During The Day	
Vyana affirmation—five minutes three times per day: before breakfast, before lunch, and before dinner	75
Practice	
Legs Up the Wall—five minutes	127
Kapalabhati Kriya—thirty seconds for two rounds	87
Breath liberation exercises	113
Feel: breath of joy—ten breaths	76
Discover *vyana*—three rounds of ten breaths	72
Visualisation: heart breathing—ten minutes	73
Anuloma Viloma—eleven rounds	24
The Surrendered Breath long practice	134

Week 4: Getting Acquainted with *Apana*

This is *apana* week. It's time to let go of stuff that does not serve you and is holding you back. By energising and liberating *apana*, mental and physical waste will effortlessly fall away like leaves dropping off the trees in autumn.

Prepare Yourself

- Read the chapter on *apana vayu* again and answer the "Let's Check In" questions.
- Note your weak points and resolve to do at least one action this week to get more connected to *apana*.
- Write your *apana*-expanding goal.
- Get more *apana*-rich foods. Write down the changes you are going to make to your diet this week.

Seven-Day *Apana Vayu* Daily Practice

	Page
During the Day	
Apana affirmation—five minutes three times per day: before breakfast, before lunch, and before dinner	89
Practice	
Legs Up the Wall—five minutes	127
Feel: *Kapalabhati Kriya*—twenty seconds for three rounds	87
Breath liberation exercises	113
Visualisation: grounding—ten minutes	87

Discover *apana*—three rounds of ten breaths	86
Anuloma Viloma—eleven rounds	24
The Surrendered Breath long practice	134

Week 5: Getting Acquainted with *Udana*

This is *udana* week. If you have been following the program and doing your daily practice, you will be feeling stronger, more energised, and creative. You should also be feeling more relaxed and sleeping better. *Udana* is the sum total of the energy forces of the other four *vayus* you have been working on over the past four weeks.

Prepare Yourself

- Read the chapter on *udana vayu* again and answer the "Let's Check In" questions.
- Note your weak points and resolve to do at least one action this week to get more connected to *udana*.
- Write your *udana*-expanding goal.
- Get more *udana*-rich foods. Write down the changes you are going to make to your diet this week.

Seven-Day *Udana Vayu* Daily Practice

	Page
During the Day	
Choose a mantra or a positive joyful song and sing to your heart's content	100
Udana affirmation—five minutes three times per day: before breakfast, before lunch, and before dinner	101
Practice	
Legs Up the Wall—ten minutes	127
Kapalabhati Kriya—twenty seconds for two rounds	87
Breath liberation exercises	113
Discover *udana*—three rounds of ten breaths	98
Visualisation: *ujjai*—five minutes	99
Feel: *Bhramaree*—five minutes	100
Anuloma Viloma—eleven rounds	24
The Surrendered Breath long practice	134

Chapter 13

The Practice Recipes

"The secret of genius is to carry the spirit of the child into an old age which means never losing your enthusiasm"

—Aldous Huxley

These recipes are ideal if the five-week plan seems a little daunting too start with, but like all things, they will only work if you actually do them. I mean daily or at least five to six days per week over a period of at least thirty days. Choose one and stick to it rather than dart around doing one on one day and another on another day. Practice requires consistency over time if it is to make a difference.

You will find video resources for the exercises at www.breathebetter sleepbetter.co.uk.

General Health and Well-being

Always try to maintain an equilibrium through a disciplined daily practice that includes cleansing and opening energy pathways, making space for the breath, slowing down the mind, balancing the masculine and feminine energies, and bringing in more *prana*.

	Page
Kapalabhati Kriya—twenty seconds for two rounds	87
Breath liberation exercises	113
Legs Up the Wall—ten minutes	127
Anuloma Viloma—eleven rounds	24
The Surrendered Breath short practice—ten minutes	134

Insomnia

Slow down the racing mind with a gentle inversion and serotonin-promoting *Bhramaree* breath. The inversion also promotes *udana vayu*, the energy that takes you into deep sleep. The Surrendered Breath will completely relax the system. *Chandra Bhedi* will promote the cooling, relaxing, and quietening lunar energy. Practice every night for thirty days.

	Page
Legs Up the Wall—ten minutes	127
The Surrendered Breath long practice—thirty-five minutes	134
Chandra Bhedi—five minutes	26
Bhramaree breath—ten minutes	100
Sit quietly for five minutes and then go to bed	

Woken Up in the Middle of the Night and Can't Get Back to Sleep

Drink a small cup of chamomile or some other relaxing tea. Go back to bed. *Brahmaree* breath will quiet the mind, and the *pranic* bath will melt away any tension and frustration. You will more than likely go back to sleep.

	Page
Bhramaree breath—ten minutes	100
The *pranic* bath until you fall asleep	134

Exhaustion/Simply Too Much Going On

A gentle inversion will quiet the mind and refresh the circulatory system.

	Page
Legs Up the Wall—ten minutes	127
The Surrendered Breath long practice—thirty-five minutes	137

Pick-me-up for a Night Out

If you are not sure how you are going to get through a night out, a gentle inversion and a *pranic* bath will refresh you and give you the energy to see you through into the late evening.

	Page
Legs Up the Wall—ten minutes	127
Pranic bath—twenty minutes	131

Bad Digestion

Energising the cleansing system and releasing *apana* will help with digestion. Pay attention to what you are putting into your stomach, and make sure you are not eating late at night. Do not drink anything for at least thirty minutes before you eat and for thirty minutes after you eat, making sure you are not diluting digestive juices.

	Page
Kapalabhati Kriya—twenty seconds for three rounds	87
Katichakrasana—three sets	120
The Surrendered Breath long practice—thirty-five minutes	134
Samana visualisation—ten minutes	58
Savasana—ten minutes	140

Depression and Feeling Lost

Vyana vayu is the best available antidepressant. Opening the energetic channels will release the mind and get you moving.

- Breath of joy—ten rounds
- *Vyana* visualisation—three rounds
- The Surrendered Breath long practice—thirty-five minutes

Migraines and Headaches

Often migraines and headaches are the result of stress, lack of sleep, and too much running. Legs Up the Wall will quiet the mind. The cleansing breath will help release mental and physical stress, and the Surrendered Breath practice will energise you with fresh *prana*. Drink plenty of water.

	Page
Legs Up the Wall—ten minutes	127
The Surrendered Breath complete long practice—thirty-five minutes	134

Stress and Anxiety

A gentle inversion will quiet the mind and refresh the circulatory system while the cleansing breath will help you release stress. The Surrendered Breath practice will bring in the fresh and new and energise your system, and the *Brahmaree* breath will free your mind of all that internal chatter and worry.

	Page
Legs Up the Wall—ten minutes	127
Brahmaree breath—ten minutes	100
The Surrendered Breath complete long practice—thirty-five minutes	134

Feeling of Shortness of Breath or Can't Breathe

A gentle inversion will quiet the mind and refresh the circulatory system. The breath liberation practice will help make space for deeper and fuller breathing. *Bhramaree* will encourage full exhalation, resulting in deeper inhalation as well as releasing stress and promoting serotonin. The *pranic* bath will encourage full, deep breathing.

	Page
Kapalabhati Kriya—twenty seconds for two rounds	87
Breath liberation practice	113
Legs Up the Wall	127
Bhramaree—five minutes	100
The Surrendered Breath long practice—twenty-five minutes	134

Morning Pick-me-up

If you have woken up exhausted, awaken your system with energy channel cleansing, liberating the breathing apparatus with the breath liberation practice. Get in touch with *vyana vayu* through the breath of joy and fill yourself up with fresh *prana* for the day with the *pranic* bath. The *Surya Bhedi* practice will encourage the solar, energetic energy from the sun to get you into action for the day.

	Page
Kapalabhati Kriya—twenty seconds for three rounds	87
Breath liberation practice	113
Breath of joy—ten rounds	74
Pranic bath short practice—ten minutes	134
Surya Bhedi—five minutes	26

Dictionary of Terms

- Acne rosacea: a skin condition, typically with facial redness, supercial dilated blood vessels on facial skin and spots
- Allopathic: mainstream medicine
- *Anuloma Viloma*: alternate nostril breathing
- *Asana*: yoga postures
- Astral planes: beyond the physical world
- Atherosclerosis: thickening of the artery walls
- Autonomic nervous system: a system that controls, largely unconsciously, bodily functions
- *Bhramaree*: bumblebee breathing
- Calcitonin: a naturally occurring hormone that helps regulate calcium levels in your body
- Chakra: a term meaning "wheel" or "disk" in Sanskrit and in this context refers to concentration of energy in particular points all over the body
- *Chandra Bhedi*: sun breathing
- Hanuman: Hindu monkey god
- Hashimoto's thyroiditis: a condition where the immune system attacks its own thyroid
- Higher self: the deeper part of you, the eternal omnipresent self, or your inner intelligence
- Hypnogogic: a transitional state between wakefulness and sleep

- *Kapalabhati Kriya*: cleansing breathing exercise
- *Kumbhaka*: breath retention
- *Kundalini Shakti*: a latent female spiritual energy dormant at the base of the spine
- Meridians: energy paths
- *Nadis*: energy paths
- Oxytocin: hormone associated with love and touch
- Parasympathetic: the part of the automatic nervous system that calms you down
- *Prana*: life force energy
- *Pranayama*: breathing exercises
- *Pranic* bath: surrendered breath breathing exercise
- Qi Gong: Chinese health-care system
- *Ramayana*: Ancient Sanskrit poem about life in India
- Reiki: healing system using energy
- *Rig Veda*: oldest Sanskrit scripture dating back to approximately 1500 BC
- *Savasana*: corpse relaxation pose
- Selenium: nutrient associated with better sleep
- Shiva: patron saint of yoga, represents consciousness and the destruction of the ego
- Solar plexus: network of nerves located in the abdomen
- Surrendered Breath: breathing technique
- Sushumna: central energy channel running from the root of the body to the crown of the head
- Triiodthyronine: thyroid hormone
- Tryptophan: amino acid from which serotonin is made in the body
- *Ujjai*: ocean-sounding breath
- *Vairagaya*: concept of surrender and nonattachment
- *Vishnu Mudra*: hand position used for breathing exercises

Resources

Bibliography

Fahri, Donna. *The Breathing Book*. New York: St Martins Griffin, 1996.

Faulds, Danna. *Go In and In*. Virginia: Peaceable Kingdom Books, 2002.

———. *Prayers to the Infinite*. Virginia: Peaceable Kingdom Books, 2004.

Feuerstein, Georg. *The Shambhala Encyclopedia of Yoga*. Shambhala Publications, 2000.

———. *The Yoga Tradition*. Hohm Press, 2008.

Frawley, David. *Yoga and Ayurveda*. Delhi: Motilal Banarsidass Publishers PVT Ltd., 2008.

Kaminoff, Leslie. *Yoga Anatomy*. Human Kinetics Publishers, 2012.

Koch, Liz. *The Psoas Book*. Guinea Pig Publications, 2012. Lancaster, Judith. *Relax and Renew*. Berkeley, Calif.: Rodmell Press, 1995.

Panwar, Chetana and Yogi Vishvketu. *Moving into Bliss with Yoga*. 2007.

Roche, Lorin. *The Radiance Sutras*. Sounds True, 2014.

Saradananda, Swami. *The Power of the Breath*. London: Duncan Baird Publishers, 2009.

Sen-Gupta, Orit. *Vayu's Gate, Yoga and the Ten Vital Winds*. Vijnana Books.

Internet Resources

1   "Breathing," accessed April 8, 2015, https://en.wikipedia.org/wiki/Breathing.

2   Department of Physiology at the Jawaharlal Institute of Postgraduate Medical Education and Research in Pondicherry, India, "Health Benefits of Slow Breathing Resources," *Indian J Med Res* 120 (August 2004): 115–121, accessed April 8, 2015, http://medind.nic.in/iby/t04/i8/ibyt04i8p115.pdf.

3   The Heart Foundation, http://www.theheartfoundation.org/heart-disease-facts/heart-disease-statistics; World Health Organisation, http://www.who.int/cardiovascular_diseases/resources/atlas/en.

4   "Earthing: Health Implications of Reconnecting the Human Body to the Earth's Surface Electrons," accessed April 8, 2015, http://www.ncbi.nlm.nih.gov/pmc/articles/PMC3265077.

5   "Triangle of death (Italy)," accessed April 8, 2015, https://en.wikipedia.org/wiki/Triangle_of_death_(Italy).

6   "Lung volumes," accessed April 8, 2015, https://en.wikipedia.org/wiki/Lung_volumes.

7   "Effect of short-term practice of breathing exercises on autonomic functions in normal human volunteers" (http://www.ncbi.nlm.nih.gov/pubmed/15347862) shows the effect of short-term practice of breathing exercises on autonomic functions in normal human volunteers. The increased parasympathetic activity and decreased sympathetic activity were observed in slow breathing group, whereas no significant change in autonomic functions was observed in the fast breathing group. "Effects of mental relaxation and slow breathing in essential hypertension" (http://www.ncbi.nlm.nih.gov/pubmed/16765850) shows even a single session of mental relaxation or slow breathing can result in a temporary fall in blood pressure. Both the modalities increase the parasympathetic tone but have effects of different intensity on different autonomic parameters.

Printed in the United States
By Bookmasters